George Verwer, Founder of Operation
"I am excited about this book, but its 50 ye.
over 50 years ago I have been urging peopl
must be whether they come to know him or not. We are paying a heavy price for our alienation, prejudice and lack of action. Now in London alone we have about one million Muslims. What a huge joy to know that some are coming to Jesus and we must go the extra mile to love them, encourage them and work with them in any way possible. This important amazing book can help us do just that. Please don't just read it, but get copies to give to others."

Greg Livingstone, Founder of Frontiers.
"Tim and Rachel Green have lived years in Muslim countries. His Ph.D. addresses the vital issues of identity for those who have been rejected by their biological families who hunger for what our Heavenly Father intends Christ's family to be for them. Roxy is one of those precious jewels whom Christ Jesus adopted, who herself has gone through the crucible of rejection by her clan but eventually found a family among Christ's disciples in Britain.

Reading it brought me hope that herein is vital guidance which Christians in the West need who have longed to know how to keep connected with and serve Muslim background Christians who desperately need to be adopted into and nurtured by Christ's family.

Spend time in the "points to ponder", and interact with like-minded welcomers of those who pay the terrible price of 'betraying their families' by entering Christ's family.

Admittedly, it is not often that I, as a veteran focused on the rescue mission of Muslims for over fifty years, read a book that takes me into further understanding of what it means to 'make disciples' (among Muslims). Joining the Family did just that. It generates two wishes: One, that it will be absorbed by God's people who are motivated to effectively love their brethren cast out of their Muslim families and two…that this book would have been produced and widely distributed decades ago!"

Vaughan Roberts, Rector of St Ebbe's and Director of Proclamation Trust
"This excellent book is just what the church needs to help us catch up with the remarkable work God is doing in bringing people from Muslim backgrounds to Christ and to equip us to play our part in helping them grow with us as fellow members of his family."

JOINING
- THE -

family

Welcoming Christ's followers of Muslim background into his community

TIM GREEN AND ROXY

2016

INTERSERVE

Joining the Family

© 2016 Tim Green & Roxy

First Edition 2016

Unless otherwise stated, Scriptural quotations in this publication are from the Holy Bible, New International Version, copyright © 1973, 1978, 1984, 2011 by the International Bible Society.

Published by Kitab - Interserve Resources
5/6 Walker Avenue, Wolverton Mill, Milton Keynes MK12 5TW
Email: sales@kitab.org.uk
www.kitab.org.uk

British Library Cataloguing in Publication Data
A catalogue record for this book is available from the British Library
ISBN: 978-0-9928610-5-6

Cover photo: © Mint Images Limited / Alamy Stock Photo
The people depicted on the cover are models.

Graphic design by Heather and Mark Knight
Cover design by Heather Knight and Huw Briscoe
Printed and bound by The Lavenham Press Ltd

Dedication

You are a chosen people.
You are royal priests, a holy nation,
God's very own possession...
Once you had no identity as a people;
now you are God's people.
(1 Peter 2:9-10)

Family isn't always blood.
It's the people in your life who want you in theirs:
the ones who accept you for who you are...
(Unknown)

To those who have lost blood family and those who have accepted
believers of Muslim backgrounds into their own family.

And to our own families.

Acknowledgements

We want to thank the Lord Jesus Christ for all that he has done in our lives and in the lives of many Muslims who have chosen to follow him as Lord.

We want to thank the *Joining the Family* core group for the time we've spent together forming the vision and all the work they have put into the course and seminars. Thank you for the privilege and opportunity to write this book. We have been inspired and blessed by your support and encouragement as we have worked on this material.

We thank Christ's followers of diverse Muslim backgrounds who played a huge part in shaping this book: directly through your many quotes included, and indirectly because your lives have influenced our thinking. You are dear friends and we thank God for you.

We also thank the many other people who have contributed comments and ideas for this book. This is the book it is because of your insights and wisdom. Thanks for taking the time to read it and for sharing honest, helpful thoughts with us.

We thank Interserve and Mahabba for their support and for publishing these materials. And to our editor Rebekah Lees, thanks for your help in improving the raw material and making it readable. And for the cover and internal design we'd like to thank Mark and Heather Knight and Huw Briscoe from Unfold Studio for the cover typography. We really appreciate the collaboration effort of all those involved in making this book attractive and readable.

I, Tim, want to thank Rachel, my wife of more than thirty years. Your heart like mine is for those of Muslim heritage who became our brothers and sisters in Christ; you have modelled family to them and have welcomed them into our home. Thanks too to our three children who extended love to friends like 'Uncle Isa'.

Last but no means least I, Roxy, want to thank my husband for supporting me throughout this process and putting up with my obsession with the *Joining the Family* project in the last few years. You are my soul mate and my best friend and my greatest encourager! And my family who showed me so much of God's father heart when they adopted me into their own family. I love you and without you I know I couldn't have written this book.

Contents

Joining the Family

Foreword

It's a privilege to be able to commend this remarkable book, and I can think of many reasons why it deserves a wide circulation.

It really is the first of its kind in addressing in some depth all the different issues about how believers from Muslim backgrounds can be integrated into the life of Christian communities. Those who have appreciated the Friendship First course and understood what's involved in relating to Muslims and sharing the gospel with them will be glad to explore the next stage – which can sometimes be very much harder – of helping new believers in their journey of faith.

It's extremely readable – with short paragraphs, many headings and separate boxes, together with helpful conclusions and questions for reflection at the end of each chapter. Producing the book alongside the video clips, the study material and a website shows that the authors have a lot of experience in teaching and appreciate the variety of ways by which people learn.

All the difficult questions – about cultural issues, life-style, relationships with birth family and community, and the sensitivities surrounding baptism – are addressed head-on and in considerable detail. There is a whole chapter on working with asylum seekers, written by someone with first-hand experience of how the system works in Britain. There is also a chapter explaining the important role of pastors and church leaders.

Throughout the book there is a thorough integration of theory and practice. Tim Green has been living in Muslim contexts for thirty five years, and having recently completed a doctorate, knows how to relate the academic discipline of anthropology to the complex questions of identity and cultural change which are so important for believers from Muslim backgrounds. Roxy came to faith twenty years ago, and speaks with great honesty about being forced to leave her Pakistani Muslim community in the north and struggling to join the Christian family. Since they know believers from most Muslim regions of the world – including for example Indonesians, Indians, Central Asians, Arabs, Iranians and Africans – they are able to draw on such a wide range of experience that the principles they outline can very easily be applied in other contexts.

I would commend this book even to Christians who have no direct contact with believers from Muslim backgrounds. If we have lost our excitement with the gospel or become too comfortable and complacent in our membership of a church, we cannot fail to be moved by these stories of people in our midst who have paid a high price for discovering 'the pearl of great price' and are trying to live under the lordship of Christ in every area of their lives. This could be a way of rediscovering how the message of Jesus can be good news for every human being.

My last reason for commending this book is that it has a powerful message for all our churches. Tim and Roxy are constantly pointing out that working with these new believers isn't just a matter of what *we* can do for *them*, but also of what *they* can give to us. We as individuals can be deeply enriched and changed by all that we receive from them, and the presence of these new Christians is already bringing new life to many churches.

I hope therefore that this book will open the eyes of many to a 'new thing' that God seems to be doing in our midst at this time. Perhaps he is saying to us what he said through the prophet Isaiah many centuries ago:

> *Forget the former things;*
> *do not dwell on the past.*
> *See I am doing a new thing!*
> *Now it springs up; do you not perceive it?*
> (Isaiah 43:18-19 NIV)

by Colin Chapman

Preface

What is *Joining the Family?*

The *Joining the Family* initiative helps churches to love, equip and learn from Christ's followers of Muslim heritage. This vision was expressed at a consultation in Britain in 2013 and was taken forward by a core group comprising Christians of Muslim background and other Christian leaders with long experience in this field. They created these resources:

- a video discussion course for local churches
- seminar materials
- a website joiningthefamily.org
- and this book in your hands.

These materials were created in partnership with Interserve and Carfax Media, with additional valued help from Elam Ministries and the Mahabba network. The resources are innovative because hardly anything like them exists, and also because they prioritise the voice of believers of Muslim background. These believers give the main teaching input in the video course and are frequently quoted in this book. The book may be read alongside the course or separately.

Who wrote this book?

We, Tim Green and Roxy, belong to *Joining the Family's* core group and wrote the book under its guidance.

Roxy grew up in a Pakistani Muslim home in the north of Britain and found Christ as a teenager. That was nearly twenty years ago, and since then she has done much to help other believers of Muslim background and to advise churches on how to support them. She has reflected deeply on these experiences, in the light of her own journey and her degree in theology. She is married.

Tim grew up in the south of Britain. More than 35 years ago he was first befriended by a Christian of Muslim background. Since then he and his wife Rachel have learned much from deep friendships with former Muslims from nearly thirty countries who are all following Jesus. They enjoyed bringing their children up in Pakistan and they still live in the Muslim world. Tim's PhD was on issues of identity for Christ's followers of Muslim background.

In this book we decided to put ourselves into the story rather than leaving it impersonal. Thus Roxy wrote some chapters, using 'I' and 'my' when talking about her own experience. Tim did the same for his chapters. Then we interacted in depth on all the chapters, so that the final result combines our ideas. We learned a lot from each other and it was a great joy to work together. Indeed, this very process modelled what the book is all about: mutual learning between Christ's followers of Muslim heritage and of other backgrounds.

For two chapters of the book, we turned to others with relevant expertise. Emily Bowerman, a Christian with significant experience of asylum issues and a related masters degree, wrote Chapter 11 on welcoming asylum seekers in the church. Emily is part of the team at Refugee Support Network, a London-based organisation which helps young refugees towards more hopeful futures by supporting them to get into, stay in, and do well in education. For Chapter 8 on life structure (and also Appendix 3), we were assisted by Tom and Judi Walsh who work with The Navigators and have much experience in pastoral care and mentoring Christ's followers of Muslim background. Tom's MA dissertation was on the topic of evangelism, conversion, integration and discipleship of such believers in Britain. He is currently working towards a PhD on BMBs and their relationship to the church in UK.

For whom is this book written?

It is for Christians who care about Muslims turning to Christ and want to help. It somewhat assumes a British church context (indeed, a white British context) and most of the examples are from this context. But most of the principles are much more widely applicable, and we expect the book will be read in other Western countries and beyond.

If you are Christ's follower of Muslim background we don't presume that your experience is the same as ours. Your ethnic origins or culture may be quite different from the believers quoted in this book, or maybe your experience of family is different, or your views on church. We have tried to reflect this variety in the book, but if you still find generalisations which don't apply to you, we apologise in advance! Please contact us through the Joining the Family website to share your view so we can learn more from you.

We have also included a short chapter especially for church leaders, for issues relevant to your role. It suggests ways you can equip and encourage any members of your congregation who are specifically called to this vital ministry.

What are our sources?

Plenty of material exists on how and why Muslim people turn to Christ, and also on how and why other people turn to Islam. This is the field of conversion studies, and the focus of many conversion accounts. But much less has been written on conversion's consequences: what happens to people in the years and decades after their radical change of faith? How do they grow strong in their new identity and new community while maintaining contact with their old community? Some research is being done in this area but little has been published. Likewise only a very few books exist on the pastoral care and discipleship of Christ's followers of Muslim background, and we have listed in Appendix 1 the ones we know about.

However, a rich source of insight and experience was available in the individuals filmed for the *Joining the Family* course. These are people reared in a range of Muslim cultures who are now following Christ in Britain, as well as experienced British mentors of such believers. Excerpts from their interviews are found throughout this book. As these are oral sources, we very slightly tidied up the spelling and grammar for this written book, while leaving the words and tone unchanged. Mostly their real names are given here but a few preferred to use a pen name.

The final source for this book was our own personal experience which in turn draws on many old incidents, conversations and friendships, half-forgotten like coins dropped in the ground. The process of writing forced us to plough up the soil and so rediscover what lay there; the memories glinted afresh as we sorted and reflected on them, and as we compared our discoveries with each other.

Islam and Islams

Someone said "there are as many Islams as there are Muslims". Others maintain there is only one Islam, monolithic and unchanging. The truth lies somewhere in the middle, we believe Islam has many varieties but they share a common thread. In any case, this book is not about Islam as such. It's about people who were reared as Muslims but who now follow Jesus. Because they know their former faith from the inside, their views carry more weight than those of outsiders. At the same time, the sample preselects for those who found something lacking in Islam. Their perspectives on Islam are important but are not the only perspectives.

A separate question is how they now view the Muslim cultures in which they were reared. Some are quite negative, some are positive. Interestingly, several who started by rejecting their Muslim heritage when they first turned to Christ, have years later come to appreciate parts of it once more. This is part of their long identity journey, from where we start out in Chapter 1 and to which we finally return in Chapter 12.

One person commented that Muslims in Britain feel "very vulnerable at the moment", being under government scrutiny and in the media spotlight. She asked that *Joining the Family* not inflame the situation by promoting a wholly negative view of Islam. Nor should it so highlight the pain which Christ's followers experience from family rejection, that we forget the pain which those family members also feel when their loved one leaves Islam. The joy in the receiving community is matched by pain in the one an individual has left. These are fair comments, and we echo them in Chapters 9 and 10.

'Points to ponder'

Some of the ideas in this book are probably new to you and will prompt you to reflect on your own journey with Jesus. For instance have you ever thought deeply about the following:

- What factors moulded your own identity in childhood?
- What things or people helped you grow as Christ's disciple? Did someone intentionally help you grow or was it a more informal process?
- Have you yourself experienced church as 'family' to the extent we

suggest it should be for new believers of Muslim background?

- What elements in our western church culture are biblical and what are not? What can we learn from other cultures in the way we 'do church'?
- If you belong to two different groups or cultures at once, what ways have you learned to handle this successfully?

To help you make such connections and digest the teaching as you go along, we have included 'Points to Ponder' at the end of each chapter. You suggest you pause on these before proceeding to the next chapter. Better still, talk them through with Christ's follower of a different ethnic background to yourself. Or take part with a group in the *Joining the Family* course where you will find much to discuss together.

Is this book the last word on this topic?

Absolutely not! This book breaks new ground. Surely some readers will disagree with what we have written, while others will want to add to it. Either way, please contact us through the Joining the Family website. Our own thinking continues to evolve, so help us by joining the discussion, and we can add your ideas to a later edition of this book or to the website.

Roxy and Tim, April 2016

Joining the Family

CHAPTER ONE

Why this book?

(Tim writing...)[1]

One evening this week, 'Farida'[2] wept her heart out in prayer. She and her husband had asked me and my wife to go and pray with them. For eight long years they have been living in limbo in a foreign country, waiting for their resettlement case to be decided. Two years before that were spent on the run in Pakistan, fleeing her father who wanted to kill her, since in his eyes she brought terrible disgrace by abandoning Islam and marrying a Christian.

Yet, surprisingly, Farida's tears were not tears of pain. They were tears of gratitude. "Thank you so much for my Christian family", she sobbed in prayer. "Thank you for this brother and sister in Christ who came to be with me tonight. Thank you for my husband who supports me so much and cares for me so tenderly. Thank you for all Christ's followers who have been so good to me in this land. Thank you, thank you, thank you!"

This book is about being 'family' for Christ's followers of Muslim background. Farida hasn't seen her birth family for a decade, and that hurts. But she has gained another family in Christ. In whichever country she finally settles, she will find a branch of that family there. I just hope they understand her needs and can love her like their own flesh and blood.

Muslims finding Jesus

In previous generations Farida's story would have been unusual. Not so today,

---

1 Some chapters in this book are written by Tim and some by Roxy. Learn more about who we are in the Preface.
2 Not her real name. In this book we use a mix of real names and assumed names for believers of Muslim background, according to each person's preference.

with more Muslim people than ever before choosing to follow Jesus Christ, as a growing body of evidence shows.[3] Admittedly this trend is uneven, with some ethnic groups turning to Christ in greater numbers than others, and with conversion to Islam taking place alongside conversion from Islam. Nevertheless the trend is unmistakeable, and it will probably continue to gather pace as the internet makes the gospel more accessible to Muslim people than ever before, and as the first Christ-followers in each Muslim ethnic group pave the way for others to follow. Moreover, the atrocities of Islamic State (ISIS) bring embarrassment to many Muslims and cause some to question their faith. But much depends on the prayers of Christians, and their response to the Muslims in their midst - including the latest influx of a million Middle Eastern refugees to Europe. Will we recoil in fear or reach out in love?

Thirty years ago, I used to work in a factory near Manchester, in the north of England. Most of my workmates were Muslim, as were nearly all my neighbours where I lived. Some Christian friends and I used to meet to pray for them to find Christ. At that time there was little response. Today, the situation is starting to change in that town. It is similar in other places across the north of England. Rev. Phil Rawlings, convenor of the Joining the Family initiative, recalls how he noticed the change:

> In November 2012, in Manchester, a young Muslim lad walked into the Cathedral and asked, "How do I become a Christian?". That same weekend a Saudi woman walked into a local church asking the same, and a young Somali lad who had befriended a Christian, was so impressed with him that he asked the same question. Since then I've come across a number of similar situations across the city, indeed across the country. It got me thinking, "How well prepared is the church for the harvest that God is bringing? For what may be a trickle at the moment, God willing will become a stream, then a river and even a flood."

This image reminds me of what a veteran missionary to the Arab world told me many years ago. He described how river beds in the Arabian desert stay dry for months or even years on end. But just occasionally it rains hard, and then flash-floods rush down in torrents through the river beds. But if there is no dam to catch the water, it all runs to waste and in no time it has vanished again. Then the missionary turned to me and predicted, "The rains are on the way, and Muslims will turn to Jesus in floods. But will we catch the precious water? It's time to build those dams!"

His prediction all those years ago is just beginning to be fulfilled. So now is the time to build the dams, not later when it might be too late. Now is the time for

---

3   Duane Miller & Patrick Johnstone, 'Believers in Christ from a Muslim Background: A global census', (*Interdisciplinary Journal of Research on Religion*, 2015) see www.religjournal.com, Volume 11, Article 10. The estimated statistics may be somewhat high (including probably for the UK)..

Christ's followers to understand, love and equip these new believers of Muslim background. This task is not about inanimate things like water and concrete dams, nor even about trends and strategies, but above all it's about *people*. God is entrusting to us these precious brothers and sisters in Christ. Some of them will join our established churches, others will form their own witnessing fellowships, but either way they are our family members. And they need our family love.

Needing a family

It's one thing for a Muslim person to begin the journey of faith in Christ, but another to keep pressing on in this journey, year after lonely year. If they are rejected by their birth community without really finding a new community in Christ, they are left isolated and vulnerable.

Not all such believers are rejected by their Muslim families. But whether or not they are, they also need Christ's followers to be a new 'family' to them. This new family can give them love, support, and a visible model of what Jesus' community looks like, while helping them grow into active servants of the Lord.

Take Hannah Shah for instance. Her parents came from Pakistan but she was born and brought up in Britain. At the age of sixteen, under threat of a forced marriage, she left home and soon after gave her life to Christ. So began a long journey of adjustment which continues to this day. Hannah loves the church and longs for Christians to understand better the needs of people who, like her, have left Islam. She wrote the following letter as a cry from her heart to her Christian friends:

Dear Family of God,

We need each other. We need family, friends, community, we need relationships with God and humans. We need to share our life with others. And God, the God of the Bible sent Jesus into the world to restore relationship with him. And then Jesus spoke about the body, the living family of God. He called Peter to be the rock on which God would build his church. We lose out on so much when we assume discipleship is just about the spiritual life. There's more to us. We each one are physical, mental, emotional and spiritual beings. It would be such a shame and detrimental to our growth if we ignore any part of ourselves. We are created this way by our Creator and Father.

We decided to convert, to change our religion, to change our allegiance, to change our life, to join the family of God, to believe Jesus as the Son of God and not just a Prophet, to take a risk of losing our families, our old lives and relationships that are important to us. We made a decision sometimes without realizing how it would change our lives and what we were risking. We didn't realize it could affect every part of our lives.

And you the family of God we joined didn't realize either, some of you weren't ready for a convert from Islam. The Christian people didn't understand the implications for our lives either. But God was and continues to be our hope and reason for living. Who Jesus is and what Jesus did is the reason we keep believing, but you also all have a part to play. We need you to support us, to be our family, to love and accept us and help us to make a new life. We are all part of the family of God! And what a family that is!

We love God and we want to be baptised, declare our faith in Jesus to the world but we need your wisdom and help to protect ourselves. We need you to be ready for the possible family difficulty, threats, and other issues too. We need you to understand that just because we became a Christian we are not used to the language you use and the decisions you make about food, culture and other things. Help us to be disciples of Jesus.

Discipleship for us is not just an Alpha course or a few one to one meetings. It's walking together the journey with each other to help each other get closer to Jesus and be more like him. It's loving each other. It's sharing our faith and our doubts. It's being able to ask questions about the faith and praying for each other. It's growing into the people God wants us to be. It's a lifelong journey. We disciple each other sometimes without realizing it; other times we are more intentional in discipleship and mentoring. Discipleship for converts from Islam is about the whole of life not just spirituality.

We took the risk of losing our family, of threats from our family. But some of you were not ready to receive us. So where do we go? When we decided to choose to follow Jesus, we did not want that to mean that we would leave the family we are part of, but for some of us that has happened. We would like to be empowered to make the decisions about our lives for ourselves, to learn from you what it means to have a personal faith, without pressure from anybody else. We would also like to keep as many doors open to the family as is possible. But we also want to part of the family of God.

Yours in Christ,
Hannah Shah

That's a powerful plea, isn't it? She asks us to open our minds to understand, and open our hearts to care. This book, and the accompanying discussion course *Joining the Family*, helps us take the first steps in doing that.

A huge dislocation

Imagine you have to migrate to another country. What challenges would you face? You must learn a new language, find a new circle of friends and, by trial and error, figure out your new culture's unwritten codes of conduct. You keep asking yourself, "How will I fit in? How long will it take me to feel at home in this new land?" And meanwhile you are mourning the loss of all you left behind. It's a huge dislocation, isn't it?

In 1900, a Romanian Jew called Marcus Eli Ravage migrated to the United States. Many years later he wrote his story, *An American in the Making*, to help his readers grasp why migration triggers such a massive identity transition:

> If you would get a glimpse of the pathos and the romance of readjustment you must try to put yourself in the alien's place. And that you may find hard to do (...) Try to think of the deep upheaval of the human soul, pulled up by the roots from its ancient, precious soil, cast abroad among you here, withering for a space, then slowly finding nourishment in the new soil, and once more thriving (...) If you can see this you may form some idea of the sadness and the glory of his adventure.

> If I could bring home to you even the smallest fraction of this sacrifice and this upheaval, the dreaming and the strife, the agony and the heartache, the endless disappointments, the yearning and the despair all of which must be ours before we can make a home for our battered spirits in this land of yours...

> We are not setting out on a trip; we are emigrating. Yes, we are emigrating, and there is our experience, our ordeal, in a nutshell. It is the one-way passport for us every time.[4]

Can you "put yourself in the alien's place", as Ravage puts it? Can you see how readjustment means 'deep upheaval of the human soul'? And how it reshapes the migrant's identity over time? Seventeen years after reaching America, Ravage's identity journey was still not complete. He knew that "we are not what we were" but still felt that "we sometimes hardly know ourselves".[5]

---

4 Marcus Eli Ravage, *An American in the Making*, (Harper & Brothers, 1917), p.14-15. The whole book can be accessed on https://archive.org/stream/anamericaninmak00unkngoog#page/n14/mode/2up/
5 Marcus Eli Ravage, *An American in the Making*, p.16.

Spiritual migrants

This book is not about migration. But the analogy helps us see that migrating to a new faith is at least as disruptive as migrating to a new country. 'Migrants' from Islam to Christ begin a journey of aching but joyous upheaval which lasts for decades; they could echo each of Ravage's paragraphs above. Is it surprising then if, like Ravage, they feel that "we sometimes hardly know ourselves"?

Remember too that many (not all) of these dear brothers and sisters in Christ are double migrants. They have migrated spiritually from Islam to Christ and have also migrated physically to the West. So they undergo two identity upheavals at the same time! In practice these are mixed together. Think of the questions that swirl around for an Afghan believer joining a white British church:

- How does she work out what's British and what's Christian?
- Can she remain authentically Afghan whilst following Jesus?
- And, on the days she's feeling terribly homesick, what does she pine for most?

The 'homeland' still matters for any migrant. You can't thrust it out of your life as if it never existed. It is part of what shaped you. Likewise your new community does not simply replace the old, since spiritual migrants continue to relate to both communities just as physical migrants do. They can resonate with Ravage's words:

> However aggrieved we may feel toward our native home, we cannot but regard our leaving it as a violent severing of the ties of our life... Something of ourselves we always leave behind in our hapless, cherished birthplaces. And the heaviest share of our burden inevitably falls on the loved ones that remain when we are gone.[6]

All first-generation Christians, whatever their background, still have a non-Christian family whom they continue to love. It's just the same if their family happens to be Muslim. Turning to Jesus may have caused severe strain in their family relations, and believers ruefully recognise that this "burden inevitably falls on their loved ones" as Ravage put it. But if at all possible they want to keep some connection with their birth community while also joining their new community; and their old identity is transposed into the new without being completely eliminated.

Identity, community and life structure

Time and again believers of Muslim background describe a search for identity, "Who am I now that I have left Islam?" This journey into a new identity in Christ takes many years, and is overwritten on their old identity rather than obliterating it

---

6   Marcus Eli Ravage, *An American in the Making*, p.16.

altogether. On this journey they explore how these two identities relate to each other - and how to be strong in Christ without necessarily becoming Western.

But identity is always formed in the context of community: "*Who are we?*" Christ's followers of Muslim heritage normally relate to two communities at the same time: their new community of Christ's followers and their birth community which is Muslim. Just because they have found new family in Christ doesn't mean that they abandon all ties to their old family whom they still love deeply and whom God loves too. These two communities may be socially separate or they may overlap somewhat (e.g. when other family members have come to faith), but in both cases the issues of dual belonging need to be negotiated.

Along with these interlocking themes of *identity* and *community*, arises the question of *life structure*. Islam's structured way of life provides guidance from morning to night and from the cradle to the grave. When a person nurtured in this framework turns to Christ, they may feel relieved to be no longer bound by the detail. But this may also generate anxiety, "What am I supposed to do with all this freedom?" So, what kind of framework can help this new believer grow as Christ's disciple but without imposing a system of man-made rules? And what valuable aspects of Muslim culture may helpfully be retained in the new life structure?

These themes of identity, community and life structure keep recurring through this book and provide most of its chapter headings. It's important for us as Christians to understand these themes so that we can support our friends of Muslim heritage to explore their new identity in Christ, to find community among his people and to choose their own frameworks for life.

Terminology and models of church

Unfortunately, a polarised debate in some Muslim-majority countries has spilled over into our western context without recognising the different setting. Actually, we think the debate itself needs reframing for a western context where Muslims are the minority, not the majority, in a host culture.

The discussion swirls around two points in particular:

a) Terminology. Certain terms have taken on different loaded meanings. In some circles the word 'convert' is used for someone totally extracted from their Muslim community, and 'Muslim follower of Christ' for someone still embedded within it. Missionaries disagree over which approach is better, or whether there is a middle way. In this book we use the phrase 'believer of Muslim background' (shortened to BMB) rather than MBB ('Muslim background believer') because this is what these believers themselves mostly prefer. But we mix this with other terms and we avoid taking sides in the debate.

b) Models of Christ's community. We don't take sides on this either. Some argue that Christ's followers of Muslim heritage should form their own worshipping groups, while others advocate integration into existing churches. We believe that it depends on the situation. The biggest need is to find a 'family' of fellow-believers. Sometimes this will happen by being welcomed into an existing church (whatever its denomination or ethnic mix), sometimes by linking up with other same-background believers, and often with a combination of both models. By understanding the underlying principles we can help our friend of Muslim background find what works best for them, rather than imposing on them a pre-planned solution.

A two-way blessing

I wrote above that it's time to "understand, love and equip" believers of Muslim background. But that's only half the story. It suggests a flow of blessing in one direction, *from* the churches to Christ's followers coming from Islam; but shouldn't blessing flow in the other direction too? Don't our churches in the West desperately need the new infusions of spiritual energy and theological insight which come from Christians of other backgrounds? Already half the regular Christian worshippers in London are non-white. Already Iranian ex-Muslims are among the largest ethnic minorities in the Church of England, and already they are producing ordained ministers like my friend Rev. Mohammad in Liverpool. (Can 'Rev.' and 'Mohammad' go together? Why not?!). Already Iranians and Afghans are being baptised in large numbers in Germany, the Netherlands and Scandinavia. Already in France North African believers of Muslim background in their thousands are strengthening the churches and its leadership. Already in the United States evangelists like Nabeel Qureshi are making an impact for Christ. It's happening already. Christians of Muslim background are contributing fresh life to our churches. And it's just the start.

Speaking personally, my life has been hugely enriched by the scores of people I have met from more than thirty countries who were born into Islam but now follow Jesus Christ. I count some of them among my closest friends and I have learned so much from them.

So the aims of this book are not merely to understand, love and equip believers of Muslim background - but also to learn from them.

The big vision

Above all, what excites us is this: in our day, for the first time in history, believers of Muslim background are becoming a significant stream in the world Christian movement! What we have seen so far is just the beginning, the firstfruits of that great harvest celebrated in heaven's praises:

You were slain, and with your blood you purchased for God
Persons from every tribe and language and people and nation.[7]

But in a generation's time, will the stream still be growing stronger? Will today's believers be multiplying the message through their Muslim friends and families? Will they form strong marriages in Christ and nurture their children in a firm identity (even where the tide of secularism sucks so strongly)? Will they create a new cultural fusion of what's best in Muslim cultures with what's best in the West, all under the lordship of Christ? Will the world church make room for them, learning humbly from them as well as sharing with them our heritage of faith?

And will each one of us, today, play our small part in this vision? Will we love, encourage and equip that precious believer of Muslim background whom Jesus has entrusted to us?

POINTS TO PONDER:

Consider the following questions and jot down your ideas.
Discuss them with someone else if you wish.

1 What do you understand to be the main purposes of this book?

2 In what ways do you think that turning from Islam to Christ is like migrating from one country to another? In what ways is it different?

3 Does the 'big vision' at the end of this chapter excite you? Is it in line with your own vision?

---

7   Revelation 5:9, NIV.

Joining the Family

CHAPTER TWO

Birth community

(Roxy writing…)

> Identity and community are linked in traditional societies. In the individualistic West, if I ask "who are you?" you'll probably say, "Oh, I'm a teacher" or "I work in a bank". But if I ask someone in a more traditional society "who are you?" they might reply "I am Ahmad son of Khalil son of Rafiq, of the so-and-so clan of the so-and-so tribe, and we came to live in this valley 500 years ago". They don't answer as an individual but by the group they belong to and its heritage. Which is why an Arab proverb says "if you want to know who I am, ask who we are".[1]

I was born and brought up in a Pakistani community in Britain. It was a small community and most people were from the Punjab in Pakistan rather than Mirpur in the Pakistani controlled part of Kashmir, which is where the majority of Muslims are from in Britain. My brothers and sisters and our friends were all the second generation making our home in the UK from within our families. Therefore there were no tried and tested methods of integration into the culture that we could draw on. We were learning what did and didn't work for us as we grew up. It felt like we had to switch between one world and another: the world of home and Pakistani Muslim community, and the world outside of the Muslim community - of school and elsewhere. We learnt from a young age what acceptable behaviour was and how to interact with people. For example, it was acceptable to talk to people of the opposite gender at school and elsewhere outside of the Muslim community; in fact it was rude if you didn't. But at home and in the Muslim community interactions with the opposite gender outside of your biological

---

1   Tim Green in the *Joining the Family* course.

family were frowned upon and could dishonour the family.

The effect this had on relationships within the family and community was important as this also affected how believers from Muslim backgrounds, born and brought up in the UK, would relate to their family and Muslim community after they come to faith. Muslim parents responded in different ways to this switching between two cultures that their children resorted to – either, like my parents, they became protective and constantly reminded their children of the culture of the country they migrated from; teaching them about Islam OR they empowered and encouraged integration into modern British culture by allowing their children to wear western clothes, trusting them to explore their own expressions of Islamic faith and encouraging them in their education. Parents who did the latter risked becoming the subject of gossip, and therefore shame, within the community so there were very few parents willing to take this approach.

That was my experience in a Pakistani community growing up in the 80s. Things are slowly changing in Muslim communities around the UK. Pakistani communities have evolved into more settled, distinct and sometimes very conservative, communities with Arab influences such as the *niqab* and *hijab* clothing that women have started to wear. Other Pakistani families are moving out and away from the larger Muslim community since they are successful in their careers and choose a life away from the scrutiny of the rest of the community. There are a growing number of young people going to University, and life away from home gives them an encounter with Islam that is potentially more intentional in practice. On the other hand, University may give them a new freedom to explore a more western lifestyle and to explore other faiths including Christianity.

Muslim people who have immigrated to Britain in recent years have become integrated into the Muslim community without effort on their part. They clearly belonged to the community in their home country and unless they did anything significant to bring shame they had a good reputation within the community. Many Muslims would have arrived believing that the UK is a Christian country as Christianity is western and history has taught them this. And then when they come to the UK it's a shock to see how secular British society is and how individualistic the culture is, including the Christian community. The behaviour of people in the society, the way people dress and the disrespect for elders they see is shocking to them. The home countries of Muslims who have come to Britain are still important influences in their lives. When I asked Reza, an Iranian BMB, what he and his Iranian friends miss about their home country, he said:

Reza (Iranian BMB)

They miss the country all of them, you can't find a single Iranian who doesn't miss the country, not the government but the country. They miss time to be with the community in their home town. That's why many will go back to Iran many times even though it's risky. For example, one of my friends went back to Iran. He was an underground leader of the church in Iran and had to leave but after six or seven years he went back to Iran and when I asked him, "Why did you go back?" He said, "Because I missed Iran, I missed the land, miss the weather, missed the houses." The authorities grabbed his passport for six months and then they gave him the passport and they told him not to go back again. The main thing Iranians leave behind is country and close family for many of them.[2]

What family means to Muslim people

Family is really important to Muslims; not just the immediate family of parents and siblings, but the extended family of grandparents, aunties, uncles and cousins. There is a real sense that one person is only honourable if they are part of a community and so for second and third generation immigrants in the UK the lack of connection with biological extended family has been replaced with contact and strong connection with other non-related families who have become like aunties and uncles and cousins and grandparents to them, forming the community that would have naturally existed in their parent's home country. This is the family that matters to them. These are the people that make decisions together about their lives and these are the people they share life events with. They celebrate religious occasions together, including Ramadan, Eid and weddings, and they mourn together when there's a death. Sometimes they even help each other with financial problems: pooling finances in order to avoid getting mortgages so that families can set up homes.

For those who come to the UK as adult migrants, asylum seekers and refugees this is often what they leave behind and lose. They are looking for this to be replaced by a community in the UK.

Reza (Iranian BMB)

Traditionally, family has meant a lot for Iranians in Iran. People will even introduce a person through his or her family ties, for example, "This is Reza son of Naymat." And if the father has good credit the son can use his credit in the bazaar. Families value time together each day; they meet for meals at lunch and dinner, not starting to eat until everyone is there from the family. People would come home from work for lunch and then return to work after time with the family.

Now this is changing: people are not as close to their family. They speak to family once a week, as their lifestyle has changed and become

---

2   Personal communication.

more westernised. Previously, after the wedding the daughter in law would join the son's family but now the sons want their own homes and to start their own business.

Family is still important to Iranian believers. Iranian believers are looking for family inside the church, that's why when my mum used to pastor a church all the young adults used to call her mum. They were missing their own family.[3]

Honour and shame

Many believers of Muslim backgrounds come from communities where the dynamic of shame and honour is at work in the society and therefore where one's reputation is highly valued. As a noun, honour compares to our western ideas of esteem, respect, high regard, or good reputation. People describe their families as honourable because they don't do or act as others outside the community might. Accepting the cultural norms of the Muslim community is honourable. Society or community or the tribe defines what is honourable, in other words society decides what a good reputation is. Amongst the many ways that an individual can bring shame on family is by leaving Islam and becoming a believer in Jesus, becoming a Christian.

Ahmed (originally from North Africa)

So it's hard, it's a matter of honour and shame, and they think of their reputation when it comes to shame and dishonor… So they focus more on their reputation and it's hard. It can lead to complete breakdown of relationships within the family.[4]

In a shame-based society the primary way of gaining control over children and maintaining control over adults is the use of shame and the complementary threat of ostracism if they are shamed. A shame society is often compared with western guilt-based societies in which control is maintained by creating, and continually reinforcing, the feeling of guilt for certain condemned behaviours and the expectation of punishment.

In shame-based cultures, community is more important than the individual; gossip in the community brings shame. In his book *Against the Grain*, which tells the story of his journey of faith from a Pakistani-Muslim to Christianity, Khalad Hussain talks of a woman committing suicide in the village he grew up in. She had been caught in bed with a man who was not her husband. Better to die than live a life of shame! I found out what kind of behavior to avoid by listening to the gossip amongst the women in the community. I very quickly learned as a child that if

---

3   Personal conversation.
4   *Joining the Family* course

you were the subject of the gossip you were shameful, '*bey izzat*', without honour. Honour and shame are important concepts in Iranian culture too:

> This is still big in Iranian culture. We honour the elderly, their grey beard and grey hair. For example, if there is a young person with a degree who teaches students, they will think he doesn't know anything but if a person has grey hair and he starts talking then people will listen.

> There is a concern that daughters may bring shame to the family if they do something wrong. For example, my cousin left everything, fled home and went to New Zealand. This brought shame on the family and even now the family blames my Uncle and Aunt for it. Mean things are said about her. When a girl leaves home before getting married it's a sign of rebellion, a sign of bad behaviour and it brings shame to the family.

> In traditional Iranian families, someone who becomes a believer really brings shame to the family. For example, yesterday a friend told me that when he told his family that he'd become Christian the first response was, "Why are you doing this? What will all the family say about us? You're bringing shame to us, how can we live in this community again?" So the first thing for Shia Muslims is not, "Why did you do that, you will go to hell." but the first thought is, "You are bringing shame to us".[5]

In a shame-culture (sometimes referred to as honour-based culture), what other people believe is much more powerful. Indeed, my principles may be derived from the desire to preserve my honour or avoid shame to the exclusion of all else. In Pakistani-Punjabi culture it is said that one's honour is tied up with '*zan, zar, aur zamin*', woman, wealth and land.

Joseph (originally from the Middle East)
The Muslim world believes in shame and honour, and when someone becomes a believer in Jesus Christ, he really brings a lot of shame on his family. The Muslim community is holistic, so there are no boundaries between families, it is a tribal system. Most of the Arab and Muslim world is based on the tribal system. And that makes it very easy for anyone to interfere in your life.[6]

Honour comes from family lineage, religious piety, success at work, age, hospitality. For men, honour also comes from control and protection of women, land and family members. For women, honour comes from complete fidelity to one's husband and sexual purity before marriage.

---

5 Personal conversation.
6 *Joining the Family* course.

For shame-based cultures to work, shame and honour are usually attached to something greater than the individual. Honour is almost always placed on a group. This can be the immediate family, the extended tribe, or in some cases, as large as an entire nation.

Hannah (British born Pakistani)

In many Muslim cultures, the honour of males depends on the behaviour of females, and my father was a community leader with high status to defend. In his eyes I brought shame on him by refusing the arranged marriage, by running away and by becoming a 'Christian'. Shame is one of the biggest reasons why Muslim families react so strongly when their members leave Islam. Not all of them resort to threats and violence. Some just cut the person out of their lives. So conversion brings pain to the new believer but also to their Muslim families.[7]

The difficulty of restoring honour without the shedding of blood or revenge on the person or family of the person means there's very little possibility of forgiveness and reconciliation. The result of this may be that the family disowns the new Christian or threatens them with violence or even death. The family and community are affected by the decision that an individual member makes to leave Islam.

In Muslim communities your reputation, your honour, affects whether you're able to find a marriage partner:

Joseph (originally from Middle East)

When someone becomes a Christian it really causes problems for his family and for himself. For example, my niece and nephew can't get married to anyone in the community because I, their uncle, became a believer, so that has caused trouble. So you affect your family in different ways, it's not only about yourself; it is the whole family and their situation.[8]

Extract from Tim's PhD dissertation[9]

Ziya Meral argues that in many Muslim societies "the family's honour is linked to the honour of its individual members". Therefore apostasy "brings shame to the convert and the entire family" and this triggers a reaction because "a family's honour must be protected at all costs". He believes that gendered attitudes to honour make "shame

---

7   *Joining the Family* course.
8   *Joining the Family* course.
9   Tim Green, *Issues of Identity for Christians of a Muslim background in Pakistan*, (London University, 2014), p.12.

a greater potential danger for female converts than for male".[10] This is confirmed by Reisacher's fieldwork with female Muslim-to-Christian converts in North Africa.[11] In Pakistan too, the shared nature of "be'izzati" (dishonour) explains why an individual's conversion to Christianity brings disgrace for the whole family. "Auntie, do you realise what this means for other people?", sobbed Bilquis Sheikh's niece.[12] Gulshan Esther was told by her brothers, "We are a leading Muslim family, and you will bring us into disrepute".[13] Syrjänen agrees that "when a single Muslim converts... it means be'izzati not only for him but also for his whole biradari (clan)".[14]

Marriage is an important aspect of Islamic society and families take it seriously due to the connection of sexual purity with family honour. Being single or staying celibate seems to be discouraged by the Quran and the Hadiths of the Prophet Muhammad.

And one of His signs is that He created pairs for you from amongst yourselves, so that you find peace in each other, and He puts love and mercy between you...[15]

Family members will often choose marriage partners for their children when they are quite young and match them to cousins and even go so far as promising them to cousin's families at birth.

Many Muslims in Britain today are taking the responsibility of finding their own spouse and partner rather than leaving it to their parents even though the parents may still be involved in giving advice and support.

Shelina Jan Mohammed in her book, *Love in a Headscarf* puts it very clearly:

The likelihood of a Muslim talking about love in public is small. But like most other societies and cultures, Muslims are obsessed with it. In fact, Muslim men and women spend a large proportion of their time wondering where on earth to find a partner. Finding that special someone is so critical to the fabric of Muslim existence, that almost

---

10 Ziya Meral, *No Place to Call Home: Experiences of Apostates from Islam, Failures of the International Community*, (Christian Solidarity Worldwide, 2008), p.64-66.

11 Evelyn Reisacher, "North African Women and Conversion: Specifics of Female Faith and Experience." In *From The Straight Path to the Narrow Way: Journeys of Faith*, edited by David Greenlee, (Authentic, 2006), p.102-23.

12 Bilquis Sheikh, *I Dared to Call Him Father*, (Kingsway, 1978), p.78.

13 Thelma Sangster and Gulshan Esther, *The Torn Veil: The Story of Sister Gulshan Esther*, (Marshalls, 1999), p.73.

14 Seppo Syrjänen, *In Search of Meaning and Identity: Conversion to Christianity in Pakistani Muslim Culture*, (Finnish Society for Missiology and Ecumenics, 1984), p.177.

15 *The Quran*, Chapter 30: Al-Rum. Verse 21.

> everyone is involved – parents, siblings, aunts, uncles, Imams, even neighbours.[16]

For me, as for many Muslim girls, growing up in British Muslim communities, the 'aunties' gossip was the way I learned about everything in life that 'matters'. About marriage - how it was arranged, how it should take place, how the bride should behave, how the new bride should behave with her new husbands' family, how she should look after her parents-in-law and not go to work, how many children she should have and how she should look after the children at home and so on. I learned about who makes the best curry in the street, who makes the nicest clothes, who was most beautiful and who wasn't. But on a serious note I also learned that such a person down the street had run away with a man from University and that no one should talk to the family because they were without-honour '*bey izzat*', now.

It is important to remember that leaving Islam is a form of rejection of your birth heritage and a point of non-negotiation of your identity. Muslims will often speak of apostates as though they no longer exist and are now invisible to their families, to the collective *Ummah* (Muslim community). BMBs are told to denounce their conversion and their conversion is even denied. I have often heard Muslims even say you cannot leave Islam, if you are born a Muslim, you are a Muslim all your life. Some Muslims believe reversion is when someone goes back to the original former state they were assumed to be in. Since all human kind is assumed to be Muslim, if you "become" a Muslim you are only going back to your original state.

Rasheeda (BMB of British Pakistani background)

I know we do not live in a Muslim majority country where apostasy is outlawed and people are killed for their faith but we cannot be too gentle about conversion and what it actually means for the individual. The Lord asks us to carry our cross, and some of us will lose a lot for choosing the Lord. **The Gospel causes offence and Islam is being offended every time a Muslim converts. We should expect more and more offence as a time draws nearer when larger numbers of Muslims will come to Christ.** (emphasis added)[17]

Celebrations and mourning

Families and communities really come together during times of celebration and mourning. During the most important Muslim celebrations family and friends visit each other, offering each other food and drink hospitality at any time of day and night. They celebrate each other's successes together and mourn together when there is a loss in the family - either death or any other loss.

---

16 Shelina Jan Mohammed, *Love in a Headscarf*, (Aurum Press Ltd, 2014), xii.
17 Personal communication.

In Pakistani communities when a person dies the whole community congregates at the house of one of the bereaved with men and women in separate rooms. They will grieve and weep together for the person even if they didn't know him or her. This shared mourning happens over a week or two, is accompanied with food cooked and brought for the bereaved family and joint reading of the Quran in order to give the one who died an extra blessing from Allah and therefore an extra chance to go to Paradise.

This sharing of life's joys and sorrows that is such a big part of life in Muslim communities is often what BMBs miss the most. Therefore the times in the year when they know there are celebrations happening will be the hardest and loneliest times, for example, during the month of Ramadan and Eid. They may feel a greater sense of loss at this time, a loss of community, and a loss of belonging and identity. It's at these times BMBs need their new community to be extra loving and aware of their needs, they may need you to be around a little more during these times, they may need you to pray for them throughout this time for protection and for comfort. They may need you to join them for meals and invite them for meals more at this time than at any other time in the year. Or it may be that during the months of Lent or Advent you invite your friend from a Muslim background to share meals together or extra times of prayer and fellowship.

Islam the ideology and the faith

The way that Islam is taught is very different to the way that we learn as disciples of Jesus in the West. This is partly because most Muslim cultures are authoritarian in their approach to education. There's a respect for the community leader, the Imam, which results in seeing his word as the law and therefore obedience to him and his rule is the way Islam is practiced rather than an individual seeking to study and increase his knowledge and practice of Islam. Sometimes this results in practice which is based on tradition and cultural understanding rather than on Islam in the Quran. It may even be contradictory to the Islam we read about in the Quran.

Hannah Shah

In the school library I saw an English translation of the Quran but I knew dad wouldn't allow me to read it. Dad insisted the Quran, as rendered in Arabic, was the exact recording of Allah's words. Translation was corruption, and the Quran lacked spiritual truth in other languages. The fact that none of us – Dad included - understood Arabic didn't seem to concern him. Dad had learned all of what he assumed to be in the Quran at the madrassa in Pakistan when he was growing up. He had learned this without questioning his imam and from the way people in his village had practiced Islam.[18]

18 Hannah Shah, *The Imam's Daughter*, (Rider. 2010), p.129

Folk Islam and superstition are practiced in communities where there are Sheikhs and Pirs (Holy men) assigned to each family member which involves practices of *taviz*, taking Quran verses orally in water, beliefs about *Jinn* and the devil, as explained by the excerpt from *The Imam's Daughter* below. This practice is often driven by the fear of evil spirits and the punishment from Allah.

Hannah Shah

'...my pir began reciting parts of the Quran, and I struggled to follow him, line by line. He told me that I had to recite those verses every day. Then he gave my parents two gifts. The first was a taviz, which was a small metal locket to put around my neck, containing one handwritten verse of the Quran... The second gift was a verse written on a piece of paper. My parents were instructed to cut it up and stir it into my drink so that I would ingest the holy words.[19]

Practices similar to Folk Islam described here are used amongst Muslims the world over. It's important to remember that there isn't just one Islam as there isn't just one form of Christianity. There are many denominations within Christianity and the practice of Christian faith varies round the world, often influenced by culture. Similarly, in Islam there are many sects – 80% of Muslims in the world practice a form of Sunni Islam where their beliefs and practices are based on the teachings and sayings of Muhammad, and even within Sunni Islam there are many sects. Then there are large groups of communities, mainly Iranian, which practice a form of Shia Islam. The main division between Sunni and Shia is rooted in disputes over the succession of leadership after the death of Prophet Muhammad. Sunni Muslims believe that Abu Bakr, Muhammad's father-in-law, was to be the 1st Caliph and successor but the Shia Muslims maintain that the rightful successor was Muhammad's cousin and son-in-law, Ali. Although Shia and Sunni Muslims agree on many doctrinal and ritual matters Shias give a lot of importance to Imams and Saints, so much so that they place great emphasis on remembering the death of Ali and Husayn, the grandson of the Prophet Muhammad. They even observe Ashura - a day of mourning the death of Husayn.

Reza (an Iranian BMB)

I lived in Tehran, people are less religious, but still really committed to the teachings of Islam but it is Shia Islam, the rituals and prayer are followed loosely. Islam was forced on Iranians. When I was a teenager people had already become disillusioned with Islam and government, they would swear at the government but would still keep their faith as Muslims. Most Iranians believe the Islam we have and which the government is practicing is not real Islam. But the government, they do what they think is right in Islam but they've changed other things

19 Hannah Shah, *The Imam's Daughter*, (Rider. 2010), p.83.

apart from prayer and fasting, they change it to suit their own Islam. But my family weren't radical Muslims. Dad would pray in the evening and then drink vodka after prayers. My uncles used to drink alcohol then wash their mouth out and pray.[20]

Many Iranian believers have come from a Shia Muslim background which means their understanding of Islam may be slightly different to those believers who are of Sunni Muslim background. Because of the history of Islam in Iran and the fact that Islam was forced on Persian people in Iran and the authoritarian nature of the Iranian government imposing their form of Shia Islam on the Iranian people, it is important to note that those who come to faith from a Shia Iranian Muslim background often find an immediate sense of freedom and relief when they come to know Jesus and can lay down all the legalism of Shia Islam. They will often say that they don't miss anything about Islam and being a Muslim therefore they are able to leave it all behind much more easily than Sunni Muslims. This experience of Islam may also mean that they are much more disciplined in their practice of faith, and at risk of becoming quite legalistic about rituals.

Amongst the different influences within Islam is Sufism which involves a mysticism where the believer is seeking to experience communion with God through prayer and chanting. According to Sufis Islam is a peaceful religion and they believe that they are called to be a loving and peaceful people. They tend to be gentler and often talk about having sensed the presence of God in prayer and in chanting. They are also more open to the ideas of connection with God and may be more open to conversion than Muslims of other sects.

As we can see in Islam there are many different forms of Muslim and therefore different forms of practice and different responses to conversion. Some families are well educated and parents have brought their children up to respect all religions and cultures and to integrate themselves into Western societies and learn what they can from them. These parents would still love, and maintain a relationship with their children even after conversion. It's important that we don't assume that all parents, families or Muslim communities will be angry or react aggressively towards those who leave Islam. Each family situation is different with unique relationships and unique individuals who will have their own opinions and responses to conversion.

---

20 Personal conversation.

POINTS TO PONDER:

1 What is your identity and where do you find belonging?

2 If there are believers of Muslim background in your church, do they feel they belong? How do you know this?

3 After reading this chapter what one new piece of information have you learned about believers of Muslim background? What will you do with what you've learned?

CHAPTER THREE

Birth identity to new identity in Christ

(Roxy writing…)

Importance of identity

Joseph (Middle Eastern BMB)

If someone came to Christ from a close-knit Muslim community, I think the most important thing for him would be to find his identity. Muslims feel that they are part of the Islamic 'Ummah', the Islamic nation. So when you come out of this 'nation' you need to find something else to join, because you are used to being a small part of a bigger community. So firstly they want to know what is their identity: who do they belong to, number one.[1]

As for all human beings, a sense of identity and belonging is at the core of what a new BMB needs. The issue of identity is a recurring one for Believers of Muslim Backgrounds and it's really important for them to find a place where they belong.

Hannah (British Pakistani BMB)

I lost everything familiar in such a short space of time. But I coped with it initially by rejecting everything that I'd known to be Asian and Muslim and becoming as 'Christian' as I could be (…) Over time though I have been able to accept that part of me which is Asian (…) I am British Asian and ultimately I am a daughter of God and belonging to his family, even though it has been at times very hard, is very important to me.[2]

---

1   *Joining the Family* course.
2   Personal communication. This is a shortened version of the full quote to which we return in Chapter 12.

What is identity and how is it formed?

Identity is about the characteristics of who or what a person is, but is also linked to and formed by our connection to other people in our lives, our family, our ethnicity, our religious beliefs and our nationality. Each person has a complex identity which includes: language, beliefs, lifestyle, family relations, artistic and culinary tastes, gender, personal appearance, world view, social class, ethnicity etc.

When we talk about a person's identity we are clearly speaking about who they are in their core being, who they are when all is said and done. I am an introvert, a wife, a woman, a daughter of God, a friend, a British Pakistani Christian, I am English, I am western in my clothes but speak smatterings of Punjabi and so on. Most of how I self-identify is influenced by my relationship and connection to other people in my life and by my relationship with God.

In the past, being a Muslim defined who I was through and through. I didn't feel like I had an identity as an individual. This meant I also felt of no importance or value as an individual. My identity was wholly wrapped up in being a Pakistani Muslim whose family was from the Punjab region of Pakistan. This was how I saw myself until I became a teenager which was when I went through a period of rethinking my identity – I was born and brought up in Britain and went to British schools where I learned the value of individuals as independent people having some connection with others. If Islam is (as many Muslims feel) a way of life, a moral code, a structure for living, and a large contributor to one's sense of self, so when you reject Islam, whatever you replace it with will have an impact on how you identify yourself.

For me religious identity and cultural identity coexisted and therefore when I came to know Jesus as my Lord I felt the need to reject both Islam the religion and the Pakistani Muslim part of who I was. I was left with a sense of confusion and loss. I didn't know how to define my new identity. The loss of community and all that helped me to define myself was now gone. At the beginning of my journey as a new believer I had nowhere I could confidently associate or connect myself with. Therefore I was lost to myself. I had to find myself again and redefine myself in terms of my new identity but also in terms of my new community because I was cut off from my natural family and community. In rejecting them I had rejected the 'me' I was until then.

For many BMBs it is the same: their ethnicity/cultural background and religion coexisted, therefore they find it very difficult to reconcile their new identity with the person they were before. The bricks that made up their identity have been taken out and an empty space is left so the wall of their core being is threatened. The wall needs rebuilding brick by brick…

Part of my identity was influenced by being a part of a respected Muslim family, a pious family, a family that was honourable within the wider community. You are defined by your reputation; so if your family and community help you form an identity and they then label you as shameful and a traitor (apostate), as many BMBs have experienced, you may carry these labels as part of your new identity even if it is a false identity. In addition to this, you may be disowned or disinherited by your family, which again may leave you feeling as the one who is rejected and not chosen.

There are around three million Muslims in Britain.[3] Of these, the single largest group is of Pakistani descent, relatively few of whom have turned to Christ, though their numbers are starting to grow. In the UK, many BMBs come from tribal communities in South Asia and Africa, while the largest numbers are from Iran. Thus these BMBs come from many different ethnic backgrounds which influences the way they practiced Islam since culture and religion often coexist. In many such groups the codes of honour and shame influence practice of faith and similarly faith influences culture. Each of these regions has its own unique cultural codes and norms which will affect the identity of a new BMB.

Javed (Afghan BMB)

In my life, personally, I believe that I am a follower of Jesus, but I am proud to be an Afghan. So I consider myself an Afghan, and I find my real sense of identity in Christ, so I can rightly be an Afghan and also I can be a follower of Jesus. This is something that we have to learn, that when we come to Christ, it doesn't mean we lose our identity or our culture. We can bring the richness of our Afghan culture into the mix. And to my surprise when I came to Christ in the beginning, my thought was that Christianity is a western religion, and all the western culture is a byproduct of Christianity.[4]

New identity in Christ

Once I came to know Jesus I was excited about learning more about him and getting to know him. I immersed myself in the Bible, and spent far more time praying than I had ever done as a Muslim because I wanted to get to know God. Gradually over the weeks I came to realise that this new faith in Jesus was going to affect my life in ways that I had not envisaged or thought about when I made the decision to follow him. I was very low at times and felt guilty for feeling that way as I thought I ought to be happy all the time now that I knew Jesus. I found comfort in the Psalms but I still struggled, unsure of where I belonged. My ethnicity stood out in the white church I was part of, being the only non-white person, at the time. It wasn't that my ethnicity seemed to bother them, but I felt like I was on my own trying to figure out how to be a Christian and how to reconcile that with my Pakistani background. At first I also struggled to accept God as Father and Holy Spirit. I found I could accept their existence as

---

3   The exact figure is not known, but three million is a reasonable estimate obtained by combining the 2011 census information with other data.

4   *Joining the Family* course.

part of the Trinity, but I didn't know how to relate to them as my Father God and as Holy Spirit at work in my life. Jesus however, I loved and was amazed at, and worshipped in awe of his character and works. I identified with Jesus and therefore found the verses that spoke of being in Christ and of adoption through Christ really helped me to be rooted in him and that seemed to be the place of peace and safety for me in this new journey.

> *Therefore if anyone is in Christ he is a new creation, the old has gone, the new has come. In love he predestined us for adoption to sonship through Jesus Christ – in accordance with his pleasure and will.*[5]

As Christians we carry the name of Jesus – we are people who are known by their loyalty to and their affiliation with Jesus. Christian identity is to belong to a place that Jesus defines for us. Being a Christian means belonging to Jesus. And because God sees us through Jesus' righteousness we share in his identity. By living in that place, we come in some degree to share his identity, to bear his name and to be in the same relationship he has with God and the world.

I made a slow but necessary transition from having an identity influenced by the people in my life (coming from a community where the individual person only has value if he has a family and community), to starting a new journey where my personal relationship with God shaped who I was. I needed to know how God saw me right from the beginning of my journey. I needed to know that he loved me, that I mattered to him, that he formed me in my mother's womb, that he knew the number of hairs on my head, I needed to know he cared about my needs and that he would be the rock on which I could place my everything. I needed to believe these things and have faith in God or I knew I wouldn't survive outside the oppressive community I was brought up in.

I knew that people lived differently in the white community. Just as at school I'd experienced that my individual input and personality was important in the same way, as a Christian I was valued as a person and loved as part of the community; what I thought mattered and it was OK to ask questions about faith. But this individuality also meant I felt lonely as I was on my own a lot more. I was learning to identify myself with a new community but I wasn't sure if that was possible because I was so different. My experiences of life were different. Again this is why I needed to be so sure of Jesus and my relationship with him. So whenever I had questions or felt lonely I would pray or read the Bible and I sensed God's presence with me. I sensed him helping me and therefore he identified with me and I could identify with him. I was his and that's what mattered. I belonged to him and he belonged to me.

> *But you are a chosen people, a royal priesthood, a holy nation, a*

---

5   2 Corinthians 5:17 and Ephesians 1:5, NIV.

people belonging to God, that you may declare the praises of him who
called you out of darkness into his wonderful light.[6]

We are created for relationship with God but we are also created for community so I did need to identify with people too. I needed to find a place I could confidently and safely find a home, a spiritual home but also a physical home within a church community. The small youth group I attended started to give me this sense of belonging; the more I went along and made friendships the more I was accepted there. As time went on it became more and more important to me that I become a member of the Methodist church which meant I went to classes and I was accepted as a member and was able to take part in voting and making other decisions about the church and how it was run. All of this happened over a number of years but there was a time at the beginning of this journey where I felt lost, bereft of identity even though at the time I didn't realise what I was feeling.

On the whole, I was treated by the church community as one of them but then there were times when I was asked to share my story and the response to my story left me feeling isolated - they thought me to be a better person than the other young people because I'd risked so much. I didn't see myself that way. It gained me respect but it also made me different and put me on a pedestal.

We define ourselves in relationship to others, so how I was treated and cared for by the church made me feel special but not in a way I wanted. So I think if we are going to help believers from Muslim backgrounds find new identity and belonging in Christ then we need to keep reminding him or her of the truths in the Bible about who we are in Christ and enable the new believer to explore their identity with God in a way that is non-judgmental, without making him or her feel different to others in the church.

In my early years of being a believer I was often accused, by other Muslims, of having brought shame on my family, and of being a traitor to my family, community and especially to Allah. The evil one would also accuse and tempt me, just as he had tempted Jesus in the wilderness. I found it very difficult to listen to these accusations and to deal with them; the pain they brought was buried deep in my heart. I was reminded of these accusations when I was on my own and I didn't know how to cope with them until one day I opened up to the leader of my church about this struggle and he reminded me of the promises of God and of my new identity in Christ. He suggested that whenever these accusations came to mind I should try replacing the thought with God's promise and so I decided that to make my life easier, I would write these promises out and try to memorise them so that whenever I had an accusatory thought that was from a person or from the evil one, I would do my best to replace it with a promise from God. The more I did this the easier it became,

6   1 Peter 2:9, NIV.

though it wasn't always easy. Later on someone gave me a Selwyn Hughes book called Your Personal Encourager, which was full of Bible verses for this very purpose which I found to be very helpful.

Growing up in a Muslim community and a shame based culture I was conservative in what I shared - about family, life and school - with the people around me. Especially because I was worried that people in the community would gossip about me as they did about everybody else. I therefore found it difficult to trust people, and to believe that I wouldn't be judged if I shared my innermost struggles. After becoming a Christian, it took me a long time to learn to trust people even in church. I felt I might be judged. I think this might be the case for others from the community where the fear of shaming the family and the community prevents them from trusting people.

As it was for me, so many other believers from Muslim backgrounds will go through an identity-finding journey that is unique to them. For some of us BMBs who are British born, the journey of our identity started before we came to faith in Jesus as we've had to struggle with identity and belonging all the way through our lives. We've been asking, "Who am I? Am I Pakistani, am I British, can they be fused together into one identity? Where do I belong, will I be accepted by Pakistani people in the Mosque, will I be accepted by my white friends at school?" Khalida was also born in the UK and she says:

Khalida (BMB of Pakistani heritage)

The biggest difference that Jesus has made in my life since becoming a Christian would be knowing who I am in Christ, and just knowing what my identity is. Being brought up in a western society, being born in the UK and sharing my parents' culture and also the British culture has always been a struggle, so when I did read the Bible for the first time and I came across the scripture which said that I was part of a "holy nation and a royal priesthood", that was a real turning point, and something that I was incredibly excited about, and I felt so at home, knowing that God had given me this one single identity, that was worth its weight in gold really. So for me the biggest thing was knowing who I am in Christ.[7]

The identity journey for those who came to faith in another country where they had an integrated identity as part of a community may be different. For example, Favour was born and brought up in Nigeria. There she didn't have to struggle with the questions of identity and belonging; she was part of a family and a community which gave her a sense of identity as a Nigerian woman. It wasn't until she came to Christ and was rejected by her family that she started to ask these questions about identity.

Iranian believers from a Muslim background also have questions about

---

7   *Joining the Family* course

identity but their journey is different to other BMBs. Historically, there was a strong established Persian culture in Iran where the national identity was extremely important to the people until the Islamisation of Iran in 8th-10th Century. Today it is felt that Islam was forced on Persian Iranian communities which has remained in their cultural collective memory and then forced on them again by the Ayatollah during the Islamic Revolution in 1979. Therefore there are many Iranians who have rejected Islam long before they came to faith. Now they would say their identity is in Christ but they are still culturally Iranian. They have still had to adapt to British culture and for some the question of belonging is resolved by joining Iranian fellowships.

Identity journeys of people who are asylum seekers will also tend to be different as there is a sense that their identity is on hold because they have to wait to see if they will be accepted by the new country, until then they have no place in society, no job, no family, no community and so no sense of identity. This is a very painful, lonely and difficult place to be and can take a long time to be resolved. It's only if they find Christ that they find an identity in him and in belonging to a church. In the quote below, Nigel is talking about a Pakistani asylum seeker who walked into his church congregation:

Nigel (Church of England minister)

He just walked in, and afterwards he rang me up and said, "I just want to talk". It became clear that he had a lot of issues he needed to talk through. This led eventually to an asylum case, and that meant, in his case, being detained. Afterwards he came back to Manchester from being detained, with absolutely nothing except what he was wearing or could carry in a tiny bag. So he had no possessions. He had lost his family, he had even lost his country and his friends.

What can we do as a church for somebody like that? That presents us with a really stark choice. Actually, with somebody in that situation, what they really need, is a home, and a family atmosphere, and they need a lot of acceptance, they need a lot of support to steer themselves through; effectively they need a new life in this country. He said, "I am starting from zero". That was the truth actually.[8]

Quite a number of BMBs in Britain were either seeking asylum before they found Christ, or they need asylum as a result of finding Christ, so this is an important topic for this book. Chapter 11 explores it in much more detail.

---

8 *Joining the Family* course

HELPFUL TIPS IN RELATION TO IDENTITY:

1 Allow the new believer to explore his or her new identity in Christ

2 Allow the new believer to learn from the Bible and his own experiences about how God sees him

3 Give them opportunities to ask questions and share their thoughts and feelings with you

4 Keep pointing them towards Jesus and his words

5 If the new believer wants to become a member of the church or be baptised, take this seriously and remember this will help him or her to be rooted in church and in a new identity in Christ.

6 Take every opportunity to celebrate their new identity with them

Baptism and identity

Baptism helps us all take the step and make the decision to follow Christ, to find new life in him. But for new believers from Muslim backgrounds the decision to be baptised is a commitment that they take seriously. It is a decision which they see as marking the death of the old identity and the birth of the new identity in Christ. It is a celebration of new life and of new belonging to Christ, and to his family.

In addition there is the seriousness of the consequences that such a potentially public celebration which may involve being disowned by family and community, it may involve death threats and death itself. For this reason, Khalad Hussain (a believer from Muslim background) decided to have a baptism in the presence of a select group of invited people; mainly Christians from his church but also a few white friends who had no faith. It's a decision that can coincide with telling their family about their new faith in Jesus. It can be an extremely stressful and painful time.

One day I was asked by a church leader to meet with a new believer and help her to think about whether it was the right time to get baptised and whether she should tell her husband about her new faith. I sat with her and listened to her story of how she came to faith after years of searching and reading the Bible. When she came to faith in Jesus, she found it difficult to reconcile being secretive about her new faith with her love for her husband therefore she was considering how and when to tell him. I listened and together we decided to ask God to show her the right time. At the same time she wanted to be baptised in the church she was attending; her reason for this was that she didn't feel she belonged as she wasn't able to take communion with everyone else because they had been baptised. I listened to her and understood this need for belonging but I again said that we should pray and ask God to show us when the right time was. She would one day be baptised, we knew that was the right thing to do, but "when" was up to God. I also reassured her that she belonged to God and pointed out to her some verses in the Bible which helped her.

In Chapter 10 we suggest some detailed guidelines on preparing to baptise a believer of Muslim background. These are important to check through since some aspects are different from normal baptisms. Awareness of these, especially if the person's relatives are still Muslim, will help to avoid unplanned and damaging consequences.

Summary

God has called us to be his and we have a new identity in Christ when we follow him. This is the faith and hope we are called into as new believers. Identity is important to us all and we find it crucially and finally in him who died for us and was brought to life, our friend, our brother and in his family, the church.

I want to conclude this chapter with another believer's description of her identity journey which is very helpful. She clearly and beautifully describes the importance of finding identity in Jesus Christ.

Rasheeda (BMB of British Pakistani background)

When I became a Christian, God defined for me from the very start who I was and who he was, through my initial encounter with him. Me as a child and he as the father. He made it one hundred percent clear. I had lost both my parents and so I also had the feeling of being adopted by him.

I still was in a state of mourning for my past identity and in shock about some of the things my family had said to me about being disloyal to my heritage ….so I was trying to prove my family wrong.

I see-sawed for a short while between my old and new self, still not entirely wanting to let go of who I had been brought up as, and fully step into my new identity in Christ.

I had some knowledge of the Christian tradition before becoming a follower of Jesus and never identified it as Western. I fully knew it was Eastern in origin and so this only increased my desire to keep my social and cultural identity and to retain who I had been even though my creed and religious identity had changed.

I would say that the most dramatic moment of identity realization was not my point of conversion, strangely, but my baptism (the Lord personally asked me to undertake this declaration and ensure it was done, so for him it was no moot point). It was at this moment that I really understood I was part of a new tradition, part of a new body of believers, a new Christian 'Ummah' (community), there was a washing away of my past sins and being born again literally as new creation, as the waters came over me.

As I have journeyed with Jesus through the years, he has shown me the richness of his relationship with me and that formulated a lot of my new identity and who I know I am today. I could see I was a child of God, and also a daughter. Jesus was my teacher and I was the pupil. He was my father, saviour and I was the redeemed. He was Lord and king and I was his faithful servant. He was also my faithful, trusted and loyal friend and we went through everything together. So my identity was a journey of transformation, not taken in abrupt steps, but mirror reflections of my identity in relation to Jesus and learning who he actually was. I am still on that journey today and am realizing that we are born to be like him, our creator. Our true identity is to understand that he resides in us and the Father is living his life through us. Each transformation leads us towards the true unique likeness of Christ.

It is only by God's grace and loving protection that I have managed the next things I am going to mention. To this day I retain my 'cultural' and 'social' identity, having kept my past Muslim friends and celebrating festivals and family days with them ….and during recent years I have tried to tap back into who I was by making new Muslim friends. It has made me a 'whole being' again, keeping some of my rich and nuanced past identity and yet the new me is clearly visible, shining very bright for all to see.[9]

---

9   Personal communication

POINTS TO PONDER:

1 "I didn't know how to define my new identity. The loss of community and all that helped me to define myself was now gone." Why is identity such an important issue for believers of Muslim background?

2 What have you learned in this chapter that is unique about Iranian Muslims?

3 How did it make you feel when you read Rasheeda's story?

Joining the Family

CHAPTER FOUR

Christ's community

(Tim writing…)

In 2011 God suddenly started to bring Muslim people along to a church in the UK. Its pastor Ian Jones describes how this happened:

Pastor Ian Jones

In the church meeting on a Sunday morning I saw four young men sitting opposite me. I could tell they were Afghans by their appearance. During the worship the Lord said to me, "Go immediately to them now, tell them how welcome they are, and how glad you are to see them". So during the worship I went over to the four young men and I shook their hand and looked them in the eye and said, "You are so welcome here. I was so glad to see you".

When the meeting finished, they came to see me straightaway for a chat because I had broken the ice with them. Later they said that when they came to me that morning they felt like they had met their father. So for the next three weeks they were there every Sunday morning, they would come to me at the end of each meeting, and I would chat with them, and my wife Jill as well, we would talk with them.

After a month, they said, "We've heard there's such a thing as an Alpha course. Do you run one here?" We didn't at the time but I said, "We do now, and it starts on Tuesday. If you're available Tuesday afternoon, 1pm, come here and we'll have lunch, and then at 2 pm we'll start our course". But I didn't do the Alpha course with them, I just told them about the Father's love, about Jesus and the cross, about how they could know God living on the inside by the Holy Spirit, and the four of them gave their lives to Christ. One of them is now in Bible College, the others are going on strong with God.[1]

That was the start of something surprising. The four new believers started bringing along their Afghan and Iranian friends, till there were thirty of them at church at different stages of faith. Pastor Ian is excited:

I've spent 35 years evangelising on the streets, knocking on doors, worshipping in the streets, barbecue-evangelism, and I've never seen anything like what God is doing now. So we're investing our time while we have this window of opportunity and the church is very supportive because they can see the fruit.[2]

New identity, new community

I myself grew up as an individualistic person in an individualistic culture. My individualistic gospel taught me to follow Christ as my personal Lord and Saviour. It wasn't a wrong gospel, but it was an incomplete gospel. It failed to emphasise that following Christ means not only joining myself to *him*, but joining myself to *his community*. Believing and belonging go together. Just as our birth identity was shaped in our birth community, so our new identity is shaped in our new community of Christ's followers.

Did you notice that in Chapter 3 two different believers of Muslim background referred to the same passage in 1 Peter and said how precious it was to them? Here it is again in the New Living Translation:

You are a chosen people. You are royal priests, a holy nation, God's very own possession (...) **Once you had no identity as a people; now you are God's people.** *(emphasis added)* [3]

I have seen the impact of this very same passage when meeting with a small BMB house church in Bangladesh, and the same again in Pakistan, and again with a group of Afghan believers in Canada. Each time I noticed their thrill in finding an answer to their identity quest. "Who are we?", they ask. "We are God's chosen people, as the Bible assures us! This is our identity!"

Sometimes Muslim people seek out Christ's community even before they have an identity in him: they start to belong before they believe. Initially no one went out from pastor Ian's church to seek those first four Afghan men on the streets. They just turned up at church by themselves. In the past, such an occurrence

---

1   *Joining the Family* course.
2   *Joining the Family* course.
3   1 Peter 2:9-10, NLT.

would have been extremely unusual in Britain. Now it is happening quite often.

But when a Muslim person or a new believer summons up the courage to step across a church threshold, what will they find? They will of course find a *building*, very different from the mosque they are used to. They will encounter a different *style of worship*, of which more later. They will see that the church is an *institution*, with its own routines and culture. But hopefully above all they will experience church as the *community* of Christ's followers, in which they find themselves loved just as those four Afghan young men did. In this chapter we describe this community by three different metaphors, and we explore what each of these could mean for a believer of Muslim background.

1. The church as 'Family'

We all need family. Some of us have warmly supportive families of our own. Others know only family discord, or gaps where a mother, father, spouse or sibling is missing. Our Father God longs to fill this gap! He himself is *"a father to the fatherless"* (Psalm 68:5, NIV) embracing us as his dear children and wrapping his arms of love around us. He also *"sets the lonely in families"* (Psalm 68:6), supremely through his church.

Jesus had the earthly family of his mother and his younger siblings, while probably bereaved of Joseph by the time he reached adulthood. He cared for his natural family. But he also expanded the definition of 'family' to include all his followers:

> *"Who are my mother and my brothers?" he asked. Then he looked at those seated in a circle round him and said, "Here are my mother and my brothers! Whoever does God's will is my brother and sister and mother".*[4]

With almost his dying breath Jesus entrusted his earthly mother Mary to her spiritual son John, and after his resurrection he called the disciples his 'brothers' (Matthew 28:10). The Acts and Epistles are also full of these family terms for Christ's community.

This language is very meaningful for people raised in Muslim societies, where the concept of family is more intense and inter-connected than in the West. The extended family is the cradle of Muslims' identity and provides their deepest social bonds, as we saw in Chapter 2. Family members are expected to be there for each other, to keep in touch constantly, to support each other financially and arrange marriages. It's a big commitment. You belong to them and they belong to you. Muslim families are not perfect, for they can harbour jealousies, rivalries and hurts just as in every culture. But nevertheless, as a Muslim you can't imagine family not being there. It would be like being stripped of all your clothes. So

---

4   Mark 3:33-35, NIV.

when we claim to be 'family' for Christ's followers of Muslim background, they will take us seriously and will expect a lot from it.

My friend Ali Husnain's story is told in *The Cost: My life on a terrorist hit list* (Zondervan, 2016). After his conversion in Pakistan he was stabbed and nearly killed. He had to flee to Britain aged seventeen, leaving behind his family. It was tough for him to survive without them in this strange new land, when all his life had been formed in their comforting context. So imagine how excited he was when, as still a new follower of Christ believer, he attended a British church one time and was told by the pastor "Welcome to the family". "Great", Ali thought, "Now at last I have a new family to replace the one I left behind!"

His expectations were dashed. It was a big lively church, but with such a large congregation Ali slipped through the pastoral cracks. At the end of services he felt ignored while the church members chatted with their usual friends. It's not that they deliberately *excluded* him. It's just that they didn't think to *include* him in their friendship groups. On occasions when Ali came to church, they didn't notice. When he stayed away, they didn't notice either. Hurt and discouraged, Ali later told me, "I wish the pastor hadn't said 'Welcome to the family', rather than raising my hopes and then leaving me disappointed".

Later Ali had to move to a different town where he joined a tiny church of only twenty members. Now they certainly noticed if he turned up or not! They intentionally included him in a way he hadn't experienced before. They asked him to help with practical tasks like setting up the chairs, and assisting in an Alpha course. He lived in the home of one of the church members, who became like parents to him. He told me, "I still miss my own family every day, but God has filled that hole".

There are other believers longing for that 'hole' to be filled, especially if rejected by their Muslim relatives. I heard of one former Muslim who said, "I gave up my family to follow Jesus, and all I got in return was meetings!" Meetings are fine in themselves, but they are not sufficient on their own to compensate for the kind of community BMBs knew before they came to Christ.

What is your church like? Maybe it does a good job of welcoming newcomers when they arrive at the beginning of a service, but what happens afterwards? Do those people get accidentally left out during the coffee time? Does anyone connect with them during the week? Or is it a question of "Hi, bye, see you next Sunday"?

Let us not feel accused by these questions, but rather learn from the gentle critique of Christ's followers who come from non-Western backgrounds. Pastor Dupe grew up in Africa and now leads a church in Oxford. She comments, "People who have come from different backgrounds, especially from Islam, do need more support than just being in church on Sunday". Two BMB leaders with much experience in pastoral care give similar advice:

Joseph (Middle Eastern BMB)

I think churches in the UK need to be more than 'Sunday churches'. One of the culture shocks that the Christian from Muslim background faces in the English communities is that English people are very reserved. Usually they keep the distance between them and other people. And people don't really understand that this is part of your culture, but they will feel the rejection.[5]

Javed (BMB from Afghanistan)

One of the Afghan believers was a fairly new believer, and he went to a church service, where everyone was holding their hands and they were singing a song, "We are one family, we are part of one another, we are worshipping God, we are one family". Then the next week he was not very well, but nobody from the church phoned. So when the Christians say they are one family, they have to prove that by really loving and caring for them."[6]

So, what does it mean to be 'more than Sunday churches'? Above all it means being aware of people from Monday to Saturday, especially people who lack other Christian support. Each such person, including those of Muslim heritage (but others as well), needs to know that Christ's community really is a spiritual family of brothers and sisters who keep in touch with them during the week, not just on a Sunday morning. Thankfully we have some wonderful examples of this, as will be seen in the next chapter.

'Wider family' and 'Close family'

Practically speaking, it is not possible for all church members to be fully available to a BMB from Monday to Saturday. And not all are called to it. It's helpful to distinguish between what we may call the 'close family' of a few people who take on this deep commitment, and the 'wider family' who may only meet the believer at church but should still know how to make them welcome. In Chapter 5 we explore the 'closer family' role in more depth. But meanwhile for the 'wider family' members of a local church, here are five suggestions:

1) Learn how to welcome people

Speaking as a white English person myself, we aren't always good talking to strangers – in fact, we were taught as children not to do so! Even as adults we may feel shy to approach someone of a different culture, we don't know what to say, we don't want to cause offence by saying the wrong thing. Pastor Ian had to guide his English church members on how to welcome the incoming Afghans and Iranians:

---

5   *Joining the Family* course
6   *Joining the Family* course

Pastor Ian Jones

I'm having to say to the people in the church, "Please approach them. Please talk to them. Don't be afraid of language barriers, don't be afraid of cultural barriers, they are people. They are people who are lovely to talk to and have fantastic stories. If you don't know what to say to them, just ask them their story. They will tell you their story, and you will so warm to them, the conversation will be easy from then on".[7]

Even if your friend's English language is limited, they can still show you their family's photos on their mobile phone. Or try learning to say 'hello' or 'thank you' in their language. It's a great way to affirm them. Don't be nervous about causing cultural offence, for love covers a multitude of cultural blunders. A BMB coming to your church won't expect you to know all about their culture. They will expect not to be left standing all on their own at the end of the service waiting for someone to talk with them. So just say hello. Just be human.

Ask, don't assume. One believer of Pakistani descent who has spent her whole life in England told me, with a chuckle, of occasions she has visited a church and they assumed she couldn't speak English (and "was therefore deaf as well") and was a Muslim needing to be evangelised! All they had to do was to ask instead of assuming. However, even in that situation she would prefer for people to talk with her than to ignore her altogether.

2) Introduce your friend to your circle

We naturally gravitate to chat with our own group of friends after church services. There's nothing wrong with that but it can be incredibly isolating for a newcomer who has not yet broken into any circle. Recall how Ali used to feel excluded, always hovering on the outside of the cliques? What eventually helped him was a person called James who intentionally drew Ali into his own conversation circles. In this way James' friends became Ali's friends too, until Ali could go up and chat with them even when James wasn't there.

3) Invite the person to your home

One BMB who had been attending a church for nine months was asked how many of the houses of church members he had visited. "None", he replied. I find that sad, but I'm sure it wasn't a deliberate cold shoulder from the church members. It's just that it hadn't crossed their minds to invite him. Hospitality need not be elaborate. It might just be a cup of tea. But once a person has stepped over the threshold into your home you will feel so much closer to them when you next see them at church.

---

7   *Joining the Family* course.

4) Don't treat BMBs as 'trophies'

We call it the 'trophy syndrome' when someone who came from Islam is treated as unique and put on a pedestal. They may enjoy this flattery for a while, but it can be spiritually unhelpful if it makes them feel they are more important than other Christians; and the higher the pedestal, the greater the fall.

Also, this trophy syndrome separates BMBs out as being different. Eventually they tire of being treated like an 'exhibit' or always being asked to give their 'testimony'. They may sense that church members are more interested in *their story* than in *them as people*. "I just want to fit in, to be treated as normal", Ali told me. So, when you meet a former Muslim at church, don't ask their testimony straightaway. First get to know them as a friend. In due course they will probably be glad to tell you how they came to faith in Christ.

5) Keep careful confidentiality

I know believers who were hurt when church members treated their story as public property. The BMB had told their testimony in private to person A, who then shared it with person B, and so on till eventually a stranger would come up congratulate the BMB on their wonderful conversion. "And how do you know that?" they felt like responding, "It's my story, my life, why should the whole world know?"

Also, if the story spreads out to the Muslim community, the believer will be labelled as an 'apostate', potentially making life difficult for them or putting up barriers to their witness. Each BMB should be free to choose their own time and way to speak to their Muslim community, as we shall see in Chapter 9.

So be sensitive and, if your friend of Muslim background has entrusted their precious story with you, ask their permission before passing it on to another person. Or better still, introduce that person to the BMB so that they can tell the story themselves, in their own way, if they wish.

2. The church as 'Hospital'

A hospital is a place where hurting people get healed. So should it be with the church. Of course, not all emotionally wounded people are believers of Muslim background, and not all BMBs are emotionally wounded. But some are, and church can be God's provision for their wounds to be washed and eventually healed. That's what happened to Hannah in a remarkable way...

Hannah's Story

Hannah's parents had migrated from Pakistan to the north of England before her birth. Terrible abuse from her father left deep scars, as you can read in her own account *The Imam's Daughter* (Rider, 2009).

Wonderfully, Christ stepped into this mess and rescued her as a teenager. She became his follower but still needed so much healing and practical support. Christ's community was there for her - again and again.

The church helped me, they taught me what it means to follow Jesus in the world today, they taught me to read and study the Bible, they provided for me and gave me somewhere to live. I had to move a lot because of the threats I had from my family, and people from churches gave me somewhere to live. Without them I would have been homeless and in danger.

I experienced God in my dark place, in my despair. For years I went through periods of depression. Six years after I came to faith I moved further away from my family. Finally, I felt physically safe and that meant I no longer felt a need to protect myself so my emotional barriers started to come down. I met people in a church who showed me love and acceptance. They helped me to have hope. They helped me to find counseling and prayer ministry.

I struggled with seeing God as father because of my father but I met a family who became like a family to me. They loved me and accepted me as one of their own. I felt God had given them to me as a gift, to show me what love is. One day as I sat and cried about the abuse I'd suffered, the father in the family washed my feet, and I saw a glimpse of how God the father sees me. For the first time I believed that God values me & has adopted me into his family. This one act started to change how I felt about calling God 'Father' and in his best for me.

Every time my friends spent time with me during these years, when I read the Bible, when I read books or worshipped I felt I was given the courage to believe a little more that God would heal me, to live through the pain, to face my shame and to allow God to heal me.

God has done a lot of healing in me. He has given me the strength to open up my hurts and pain to Him so He can heal me. He has worked through people in the church, who have been kind, generous, loving and they are my family and friends... They've taught me how to love and much more.[8]

---

8   *Joining the Family* course.

Today Hannah is mature in her faith and active in ministry. She helps victims of abuse. The healing she received through Christ's community now flows out for the healing of others.

God's church is where hurting people find wholeness. Yet even as we gather as Christ's followers we unintentionally hurt each other in new ways as we rub along together. This is part of church life; thankfully God has given us constructive ways to forgive and be reconciled, and in so doing to build even deeper relationships than we had before. But this reconciliation process will be new to believers of Muslim background. I know BMBs who were shocked and disillusioned when they first experienced conflict in the church or with each other. They thought, "It should be better than this!" Yes it should be, and it can be, not because Christians are perfect but because they know how to forgive. Relationships cannot be healed by walking away from conflict (a pattern BMBs may be more used to from their past) but only by pressing through to the other side. Church can be a safe space for them to see this and to learn it for themselves.

Christ's church is a healing-centre. At its heart is a table where sinners gather. They come to this table not as saints who are perfect and 'sorted', but as broken people seeking wholeness through Christ's broken body and poured-out blood. At the Lord's table we draw together, whether from Muslim background or any other background, and make peace with each other just as he makes peace with us.

3. The church as 'God's rainbow people'

Nelson Mandela's vision was for post-apartheid South Africa to be a 'rainbow people' – a multicultural society with room for all and justice for all. 'Multiculturalism', an aspiration of British governments for half a century, has now been called into question but with no clear alternative recipe for how to balance cultural diversity and uniformity. Different countries in our increasingly pluralist planet try different solutions to the same problem. Some seek a lowest common denominator of national 'values', while others impose a majority culture on their minority ethnic groups.

Faced with these inadequate solutions, can Christ's multi-ethnic church be the true 'rainbow people' where each colour retains its distinctive beauty while still contributing to the yet-more-glorious beauty of the whole rainbow? That's what we look forward to. I'm excited about being in heaven with God's rainbow people, gathered to praise him from every culture and ethnic group. Or I think of it like a great feast filled with delicacies from every land, or a rich tapestry of many colours woven together to God's glory. Bengali pastor Mohan comments:

Pastor Mohan
God is the God of all nations. When we go to heaven all the nations,

all the people, in all languages will be praising God. And when we do
it here, it becomes a piece of heaven on earth.[9]

When we can achieve this or even approximate to it, it indeed becomes a piece
of heaven on earth. I have lived or travelled in many countries. In each place I
have had the same amazing experience of connecting with people I had never
met before, but knowing at once that they were my brothers and sisters in Christ.
I have stood in worship with these family members singing their hearts out in
languages I couldn't understand at all, as tears welled up in my eyes at the sheer
joy of belonging to this amazing worldwide family!

Uniformity or diversity?

I have also visited Muslim communities in many countries. There I see diversity
of language, food and dress. But in worship, I notice a strong uniformity. You can
walk into any Sunni Muslim mosque in the world and you'll find people using
exactly the same liturgy with the same prayer cycle in the same Arabic words.
Arabic language and culture are seen as more authentically 'Islamic' than other
Muslim cultures.

This global uniformity is comforting in one way, but it means that over 80%
of the world's Muslims say their prayers in a language which is not their own.[10]
Khalad Hussain was at first surprised to learn that, becoming Christ's follower,
he could talk to God in his mother-tongue Pahari. Similarly Shieva from Iran was
brought up as a Muslim to pray only in Arabic. So when she first encountered
Iranian BMBs in Britain praying in their own Farsi language, she was astonished:

Shieva (Iranian BMB)

I thought, "These people are crazy. God only knows Arabic, so they
should speak in Arabic". And in the prayer meeting that night, I was
just so touched, because I saw like all young people, Iranians, and they
were worshipping; I've never seen that in Iran before."

Shieva was so bowled over by Christ's powerful presence that she invited him
into her life that very night. These days she and her husband Reza lead a Farsi-
medium training programme to equip Iranians in Britain for Christian growth and
service.[11]

Today in the West our societies become ever more culturally diverse. But will
this be reflected in our churches, and if so how? What will it mean in practice to
be 'God's rainbow people'? Local churches that don't think consciously about this
will remain in default mode where the majority group sets the tone and assumes

---

9   *Joining the Family* course.
10 Less than one Muslim in five is Arab. Others learn some Arabic but it is not their mother tongue.
11 This is run by Elam Ministries which has a wide impact in a range of ministries in several countries. See
    www.elam.com

that everyone else will fit in. For instance, I think of a church in Britain which began fifteen years ago as a church-plant of white middle class people. It's a wonderful church in many ways, and I'm glad that there is a growing minority of members from different Asian and African countries including some of Muslim background. But the church 'culture' remains white middle-class. Others may join in on those terms, but this by itself does not change 'the way things are done'. In a local church, the wearing of cultural blinkers by a majority group is subconscious, not deliberate. The majority don't explicitly *tell* other ethnic groups to "leave your cultures behind at the door". They just model it implicitly, by carrying on doing things the way they have always been done. That's cultural uniformity, not diversity; it falls short of God's rainbow spectrum.

In fact, usually ethnic newcomers don't mind making *most* of the cultural sacrifices when they join Western churches, especially if their numbers are small. Thus, Christians of Muslim background don't expect everything to change just for their sake. But could we experiment with making *some* small changes? These changes don't need to be seismic shocks; even little steps can make a big difference. For instance, our BMB brothers and sisters would appreciate it so much if we did not place our Bibles on the floor. That's not such a big thing to ask, is it? Tom Walsh, an experienced mentor of BMBs, comments:

Tom Walsh
Perhaps church itself could be done with a little bit more experimentation. All the while we are asking the new believers to adjust to us. But when you have a new baby in your family, who does the adjusting? Is it the baby, or is it the adults?[12]

Same-background or mixed-background fellowship?
There are different views on whether it's better for believers of Muslim background to be absorbed into Western churches or form their own separate fellowships. Actually, both models have strengths and both have limitations. If a BMB is in a white church with no friends of her own culture, she misses out on that special connection with those who know 'where she is coming from'. Same-culture groups also give an invaluable opportunity for recent arrivals in the West to worship and learn from the Bible in their own mother tongue. They also provide a good bridge to reach out to non-Christians of the same culture, in this case Muslims. Curious Muslims can come along to a safe space where there are others who look like them and speak like them but who happen to be Jesus' followers. So the message about Jesus can be heard more clearly without the cultural 'noise' in the background.

However, if someone belongs only to an Iranian or Arab group while living in the West, they miss out on the strengths of connecting more widely. Their children will want that even more and, being educated in the host country's language, it

---

12 *Joining the Family* course.

eventually becomes their preferred language. Also, the same-background groups can be quite unstable, with for example a sad number of splits in all-Iranian fellowships in the West.[13]

Actually, most local churches already offer a combination of mixed-background and same-background fellowship. The main Sunday service brings together Christians of all backgrounds, while on other occasions the youth or women or men or students get together for same-background fellowship. It can work the same way for believers of Muslim background. For instance, in some British churches the Iranian believers take part in some of the English worship service, leave for their own Bible teaching in Farsi, and rejoin the others at the end. Another model is for Iranians to attend a British church on Sunday but also belong to a mid-week home group where they can pray and read God's word in their mother tongue.

Rasheeda's parents migrated from Pakistan to Britain before her birth, so she grew up with Muslim cultural roots but with English as her most fluent language; she has always been comfortable in a white-majority school, university and working environment. After turning to Christ, she spent several years in white-majority churches before trying an African church for a while, and now enjoys a rainbow-type church including whites, Africans and Asians. She comments:

Rasheeda (BMB with mixed cultural influences)

As my journey with Jesus continues I have seen real strengths in multicultural churches for MBBs.[14] This is because there will most likely be someone there from their birth background which is wonderful for them. Then when they start to grow and mature and bring new people into the Church themselves, multicultural churches appear to the non-believer as a real diversified family of God, they appear to relate better to them. This is my own personal experience.[15]

So let's make space for different models of combining same-culture and different-culture fellowship. And let's make sure that believers of Muslim background have the space to experiment with different models of church at different stages of their journey in Christ, without feeling judged.

Here Tom and Judi Walsh describe three levels of belonging for believers. (These complement each other; the first two levels are discussed in this chapter and the third in Chapter 7.)

- First is belonging to the *large group* – a church or Christian fellowship. This group will come together for all sorts of gatherings: to worship

---

13 //Osknevad
14 MBB = 'Muslim Background Believer', which is the same as BMB (Believer of Muslim Background).
15 Personal communication.

God, hear teaching, pray together, and learn from each other's testimony of their Christian journey and experience. It is good for the new Christian to belong to a heterogeneous group comprising young and old, singles and family, rich and poor, male and female.

- A second more personal level of belonging comes with being part of a *small group* that meets together once a week or fortnight. This is where greater intimacy and trust can take place. Personal prayer needs can be shared. The Bible can be studied and discussed. The level of commitment increases as the people get to know each other more deeply. Believers of Muslim background who have security issues being visibly seen at church buildings may wish to attend a small group taking place in somebody's home.

- A third level is seen in a special *mentoring relationship* with an older and more mature Christian. In this setting all sorts of issues can be raised for discussion and prayer. Questions about the gospel and understanding the Christian journey can be asked and answered appropriately. The mentor or discipler would not only be a good listener, but would have some ideas of what to build into the life of the younger person. The relationship is not just one way, as the older person learns from the enthusiasm of the younger.
(This third level, the mentoring relationship, is discussed further in Chapter 7.)

Having these three levels of belonging can be termed 'safe discipleship.' One level alone does not bring the beautiful breadth of the Christian community. Each level has its purposes and achieves different things. Ideally any Christian wanting to follow Christ diligently would have all three types of relationships.

How may our churches be enriched by BMBs?

In a rainbow, each colour's individual beauty is retained but it also enhances the beauty of the whole. Now, for the first time in history, Christ's church of Muslim heritage adds a new colour to the spectrum. It has a beauty of itself, and it also enhances the beauty of the whole global church.

Do Western churches see themselves just as being able to give a blessing to believers of Muslim background, or can they also receive a blessing in turn? Those who come from Islam bring treasures with them to enrich the wider church. They bring *fresh insights into God's Word* because their cultural background has affinities with the Bible. For the same reason they (along with other non-Western Christians) remind us of *important values* like community, family life, making time for people and respect for the elderly. They bring *their gifts to serve* as contributors to church life, not only as active members of local congregations but also now as officially appointed leaders. Some BMBs also help the church to *be bold in outreach* as Reza points out:

Reza (Iranian Christian leader)

Because of political correctness, maybe British people cannot freely share the gospel. But someone who is a convert Christian and not British, can easily share the gospel. These Iranians who are Christians in the heart of the church, they are the key people to reach out to Iranians, Afghans, British people, and even those of a stricter Muslim background like Pakistanis, Indians, Arabs and other nationalities.[16]

These are just some of the ways that believers of Muslim background can enrich our churches. Are our eyes open to recognise these gifts, and our hands to receive them? Let's learn from Rasheeda again:

Rasheeda on the contribution of BMBs

They do have something important to share that only they can give the Church, as they are the new believers from an outside tradition. They are the ones coming to terms with their new reality and that reality has a voice. This is how the early Church communities from Judaism and other faiths evolved and this evolution did not stop a few hundred years after Christ, it is a continuum even today with the new MBB communities. Rowan Williams stated that traditions that are concerned about their own security are not truly authentic. That means a willingness to change and listen, or else become irrelevant.

This change won't happen automatically, but only if say 'yes' to it. Then in turn, our changing will release our BMB brothers and sisters to be blessed more themselves and thereby to bless us still more. We belong together as God's family, God's healing-place, God's rainbow people.

---

16 *Joining the Family course*

POINTS TO PONDER:

1 Go back over this chapter. Highlight or make a note of:

- the points you found exciting;

- the points you found challenging.

2 Some believers of Muslim background (BMBs) have excellent experiences of being welcomed in Christ's community. Give examples from this chapter or from your own knowledge.

3 If you have a BMB friend, ask them about their own experience of church, and especially how Western churches can be enriched by believers of Muslim background.

Joining the Family

CHAPTER FIVE

Being 'close family' to your friend

(Tim writing...)

Imagine you have recently come to Christ from Islam. You will need your 'wider family' of the church fellowship with its full range of different types of people. You also need the 'close family' of a small intimate circle of Christian friends who are deeply committed to you. They can partially fill the aching void if your blood family has spurned you. There might only be three or four of these special friends and they may not all be from the same church, but they are the ones who you know for sure will stand with you through thick and thin. They are the ones you can phone at 3am when you're feeling desperately lonely - and they'll be there for you!

For you as a new believer, these 'close family' members can become for you:
- *role models* of what it looks like in practice to follow Jesus;
- *guides* to explain this sometimes puzzling new community you have joined;
- *mentors* to help you go deeper with God and explore his Word;
- *friends* who won't be shocked by your questions and honest doubts;
- *pals* just to hang out with.

This chapter unpacks what this looks like in practice. Not everyone is called to this deep level of involvement. For many church members, the 'wider family' connection is all that's needed, as described in the last chapter. But if God draws you into the deeper involvement of 'close family', or if he thrusts you into it unexpectedly by bringing a new believer into your life, this chapter is for you.

The privilege of being 'close family'

I thank God so much for enriching my life through Christ's followers of Muslim background. I think of friends in Pakistan like Nazir, who has stuck firm with Jesus for more than twenty years even though he is the only believer in his family and his Muslim wife opposes him so much. He has been such a faithful friend to me. His spiritual mentor was Shahid, a pillar of strength for other converts. Shahid too had hung on in faith for many years until his wife and children put their trust in Jesus. What a thrill it was to be present at their joint baptism! And how well I remember the last time I ever saw Shahid. Riddled with cancer and knowing his days on earth must be few, he told me how confident he was of being with Christ forever. I was awed by his example. Then there is Zafar, a former Muslim who has now followed Jesus for nearly five decades. His personal example, wise insights and patience with my mistakes have made a deep impression on me.

Later in Britain my wife Rachel and I have gained many more BMB friends. We were introduced to Rasheeda soon after Christ stepped into her life in a miraculous way. Since then we have watched her blossom in faith and discover her ministry gifts, especially in evangelism. She boldly invites others to follow Jesus and goes to considerable lengths to seek them out as he directs. One Christmas Day she felt God was telling her to drive to London where she would meet someone seeking him. So she obeyed, and sat for hours on a cold park bench waiting for that stranger to turn up. Right at the end of the day an Arab Muslim lady came to sit on the same bench and told Rasheeda of her long spiritual search, and Rasheeda told her of Jesus! Would I have been willing to obey God in that way on Christmas Day, of all days?

Or what about the amazing Iranian believers whom it's our joy to know? There's Mary, who as a Muslim working in a care home had once been asked to accompany a resident to church. Walking into the service she was so overwhelmed by God's presence that she forgot all about the lady she was supposed to be caring for! That day her journey to Christ began, and later she was baptised and started witnessing publicly at a book-table in the city centre.1 She glows for Jesus, and even though we now live overseas we still feel that glow when she writes us emails like this:

Mary (Iranian BMB)

I am the happiest person in the world. I have God and he gave me family whom I am enjoying more than my own family. How great it is, thanks to him. Today you remind me how Jesus is working in my life. Sometimes I need to remember these things. Have a lovely day in Jesus.[2]

Asghar is another Iranian friend. Seeking asylum in Britain, he came to Christ through the witness of another Iranian asylum seeker. He too is bold in evangelism, and has used a Christian book-table for open air witness in Britain. He wants others to find the same treasure he has found:

---

1 Her story is told in more detail in Week 5 of the *Friendship First* DVD course.
2 Personal communication.

Asghar (from Iran)

My aim is to be a good follower of Jesus and to show his glory in my life, and to give other people what I have in my life. I've received salvation. This is the biggest thing a person can get in his life. And I want to give this, God's present, to everyone. I love to share good news with the Iranians. I'm glad to say that one day in Iran, we will have our own book-table, and we will say "Jesus is God"![3]

More names come into my mind of Christ's followers in Muslim countries. I think of Azita with her entrepreneurial boldness for Jesus, or Karim with his wise insights, or Anwar who lost his great wealth because he loved Christ more, or humble intelligent Peter, or hospitable Massy with such a big caring heart. None of these people is perfect, nor am I, and we have sometimes hurt each other (as happens in all deep friendships). But my life and my wife's would be very much poorer without them.

Of the Bible books describing the joy of these 'close family' relationships in Christ, 1 Thessalonians is a favourite for me. See how often St. Paul often he uses family language in what he writes to the believers in Thessalonica:

> *Just as a nursing **mother** cares for her children, so we cared for you. Because we loved you so much, we were delighted to share with you not only the gospel of God but our lives as well (…) We dealt with each of you as a **father** deals with his own children, encouraging, comforting and urging you to live lives worthy of God (…)*
>
> ***Brothers and sisters**, when we were **orphaned** by being separated from you for a short time (in person, not in thought), out of our intense longing we made every effort to see you (…) How can we thank God enough for you in return for all the joy we have in the presence of our God because of you?* [4]

We know from Acts 17 that Paul had unexpectedly been snatched away overnight from the believers in Thessalonica, and he left his heart behind. He felt "orphaned" without them and he prayed "night and day most earnestly"[5] to see them again. When he "could stand it no longer"[6] having no news of them, he sent Timothy on the 600 mile round trip to see how they were doing. As soon as Timothy reported back that they were standing firm in faith, Paul dashed off his relieved letter we now call 1 Thessalonians; "For now we really live, since you are standing firm in the Lord"[7]

---

3   *Joining the Family* course.
4   1 Thessalonians 2: 7-8, 11-12, 17; 3:9, NIV.
5   1 Thessalonians 3:10, NIV.
6   1 Thessalonians 3:5, NIV.
7   1 Thessalonians 3:8, NIV.

That resonates with me because I know both the joy and the anxiety of caring for new believers. I know too how it feels to call them "our glory and joy" and "the crown in which we will glory".[8] Therein, however, lurks a subtle danger of treating them as *my* disciples, *my* spiritual project, not the Lord's. I have experienced that too, and the crushing disappointment when someone crashes and I feel I too have crashed. So it's a privilege, a great joy and sometimes a heartache to be 'close family' to Christ's followers of Muslim background; and a journey of self-discovery.

Whole-life commitment

"How excruciating it is", writes veteran missionary Greg Livingstone, "for a Muslim to lose his most precious and meaningful possession - the love and honour of his family".[9] To follow Jesus Christ in these circumstances takes a whole-life commitment. He predicted that his followers might lose "home or brothers or sisters or mother or father or children or fields for me and the gospel".[10] Indeed Muslims who choose to follow him:

- may be thrown out of their homes with no roof over their head;
- may hear their hurt parents pronounce those hurting words "you are no longer my child";
- may be divorced by their spouse who, under Islamic law, gets to keep the children too;
- may lose 'fields' and other inherited property.

Several of my friends, literally, paid this price for the sake of following Jesus.

Yet Jesus' prediction did not end there. He continued with this unexpected but comforting promise:

> *No one who has left home or brothers or sisters or mother or father or children or fields for me and the gospel will fail to receive a hundred times as much in this present age: homes, brothers, sisters, mothers, children and fields – along with persecutions – and in the age to come eternal life.*[11]

The question remains, if this is Christ's promise, how will it be fulfilled? Will homes, brothers and mothers simply appear from nowhere? Or will they be supplied (as so often with Christ's promises) through his obedient people? Pastor Dupe, some of whose church members came from Islam, calls us to play our part:

---

8   1 Thessalonians 3:19-20, NIV.
9   Personal communication.
10 Mark 10:29, NIV.
11 Mark 10:29-30, NIV.

Dupe (African pastor in Britain)

Let's be the hundredfold that Christ promised them, let's offer them our home, our food, our bed, our clothes. Let them feel welcome into the family.[12]

This takes a whole-life commitment by Christians, but it is less than the whole-life commitment their brothers and sisters have already demonstrated in coming from Islam. Dupe calls us to share a little part of the much bigger cost that these believers have already paid.

In Dupe's church, this was no empty rhetoric. A Nigerian lady called Favour had arrived there after being driven away by her Muslim father who had told her, "You are no longer my daughter". At one point she was without work and without money, she didn't know what to do. But the church stepped in and became her new family. Read what this meant to her:

Favour's story

My local church here in Britain is my family. I was just accepted. It was as if I had a brother, I had a sister, I had a mother, I had a father. And recently I've found that I have mothers, I have fathers, I have brothers, I have sisters, I have nephews, I have nieces to whom I'm not related by blood but because of the relationship that has developed between us.

I have these two families on my phone, their numbers are 'family house 1' and 'family house 2'. I have lived with these two families for two years each without paying rent, I have eaten their food, I come in and the food is on the table, I just eat, and I go to sleep. I met them in the church and they have really, really encouraged me, this has become my home. So it has really been encouraging, I have really found so much love. It has been awesome.

I have a list of what people brought for me, physical things: cash, food stuffs, clothes. Practically people showed me so much love. People came to visit, not just once, not just twice, but it kept going until I was on my feet again. They never left me.

I remember sometimes I was feeling so low, and I thought, "Why am I here?", and I would wake up in the morning and under my pillow was a note, maybe with money, saying, "'Sis, it's going to be OK, don't worry, God loves you". And that really meant a lot to me. This family they lived

---

12 *Joining the Family* course

in a two-bedroom house. They had two sons, so the husband and wife and two children stayed in one room, and they gave me the other to stay in. I just don't understand that kind of love!

And on my birthday, the other family that I stayed with came to the house. They woke me up early in the morning, at 6am, saying "happy birthday" and all the children were singing "happy birthday" and it was just too much love, too much love, and it can only be Jesus!

Joining the Family course

"I just don't understand that kind of love!", exclaims Favour in amazement. Do you find her story inspiring or intimidating? Maybe it's a bit of both. Perhaps you feel "it's incredible that someone would go to those lengths for their Christian sister of Muslim background, but have I got what it takes? Could I really open my home up like that? Could I sacrifice my family's money and personal space to that extent?"

That response is understandable. It's not for me to say what each person can or can't give; God himself will make that clear as we each offer him that question. It's important to say that this kind of whole-life commitment is best shared, so that one person is not taking it alone. Also not all believers of Muslim background need total support in the way Favour did. At the start of this chapter I mentioned Mary, an Iranian lady who glows for Christ. She has always supported herself financially and found her own accommodation. But there was a time when she was deeply shaken up by needs in her life. She desperately needed another Christian lady to meet up with for prayer, coffee and advice - and a safe place to weep.

Another reason why you might feel intimidated by Favour's story is that you know nothing about Islam. But that's not the point. What blew Favour off her feet, as she recounts above, was not theology. It was love – deep, lasting, practical love. Interviewing Favour for *Joining the Family*, we asked what qualities are needed in someone to 'be family' to a believer of Muslim background. "You don't have to be an expert", she responded. "Just know God, know the love of Jesus."

It was similar with Mary the Iranian lady. My wife and I were looking out for someone to pray with her and encourage her. We couldn't think of any suitable Christian with experience in Muslim ministry. But then the Lord brought to our mind a wonderful lady in our church called Rachel, who is in her eighties. At first Rachel said "Oh I can't do that, I don't know anything about Islam". But Mary didn't need an expert on Islam. It was love she needed most. And she found it in Rachel. They started meeting up and it has been a great joy for them both.

To care deeply for a brother or sister in Christ doesn't require being an expert on whatever religion they had before. What matters is how you teach and model to them the new path they have now chosen, the path of following Jesus. If you have walked this path yourself, and you love God and you love your friend, you already have all you need to help them on their journey.

A heart of love – what is involved?

British Christian Jan agrees that 'a heart of love' is the most important quality needed in caring for a believer of Muslim background: "Not just love that is expressed by words but true love, a heart that is like Jesus' love, which is almost willing to lay down your life for your friend."[13] Let's think about a few ways to express that love practically.

1) Time together

Joseph (from the Middle East)
I can't tell someone that 'I really care for you' without sitting and knowing him. So, building relationships takes time. Maybe we will have a barbecue together, maybe we can go as friends for a movie or play football, not necessarily everything we do to be something spiritual, but having time, taking time together to build friendship.[14]

There's no short cut to spending time with your friend; it's central to the relationship. It says that you are available and willing, and this communicates God's availability and willingness too. We underestimate how important those things are. Discipleship is not just about taking someone through a course or making sure they are regular at church meetings; it's about shared lives.

Be aware of different cultural expectations about how we give people 'time'. In the West (or at least in middle-class Britain) we give time by looking in the diary for a slot to meet up for coffee in three weeks' time! In Eastern cultures it's about welcoming someone who just turns up unannounced, dropping whatever you are doing at the time and offering them refreshments or a meal. Judi explains how this works:

Judi (British friend of BMBs)
They are used to having someone around them 24/7, having their family really close, just talking about things when they want to: family just being there and available all the time. If they go and call on their sibling or a cousin, you'll have hospitality and food, and you don't have to organise that. So our British way of inviting somebody around every so often or making appointments all the time is not very helpful.[15]

---

13 *Joining the Family* course
14 *Joining the Family* course
15 *Joining the Family* course

Perhaps those of us who are glued to our diaries could loosen up a bit. Judi's husband Tom recounts an amusing case of expectation-clash:

Tom (mentor and researcher)

One specific person, when they first became a Christian, was so excited. So every day they would visit a different Christian home and knock on the door and go around, because they expected and assumed that they would be welcomed. And it was only a few weeks later that they realized they had to make appointments, and they had to buy a diary, and they had to organize themselves differently. This person said "but back in my own Muslim community, I could have visited my Muslim relatives and friends any time of the day or night, and they would have given me an open welcome".[16]

But in our culture it's not easy to drop everything at a moment's notice, is it? Suppose your friend turns up on your doorstep just when you are about to head out for a church meeting, which option might you take out of the following?

- You could push past them on the doorstep, explaining "Sorry, I wasn't expecting you" while you rush to your car;
- You could welcome them in with a big smile, mention nothing about the meeting and arrive for it an hour late;
- You could invite them in, quickly pour them a cold drink, chat for a few minutes, arrange another time to talk properly and arrive a bit late for the meeting.

That third option seeks to meet a different culture half way. Westerners need to flex a bit and 'go with the flow' of what pops up unexpectedly. On the other hand, in modern urban life we can't avoid making appointments; believers of Muslim background do come to understand that and meet our culture half-way. My friend Ali now understands that my schedule does require me to plan ahead and I'm not always free when he wants me. But he also knows that I'll drop anything for him in a crisis.

2) Laid-back hospitality

Hospitality is something I appreciate a lot about Eastern cultures. I have visited many countries of Asia and the Middle East, and in each place it's the same. When I enter a home I will automatically be offered refreshments. In some cultures this is pressed on me whether I want it or not, in others there is less insistence, but either way it would be rude to refuse without a very good reason.

It's biblical too. Do you recall the account of Abraham rushing to kill the fattened calf for three random strangers who passed by his tent? That kind of

---

16 *Joining the Family* course

elaborate hospitality seems extravagant to western readers but makes sense in an Eastern culture. The New Testament too tells us to "Practice hospitality".[17]

But this full-blown treatment of guests can all get too much, with the expense and hassle becoming an off-putting burden even in the East. That's why I like the idea of 'laid back' hospitality. I want my friend of Muslim background to feel welcome and I will always offer drinks and nibbles if they drop by. If it happens to be at a mealtime I will invite them to join in with whatever I happen to be eating with my family. It doesn't need to be elaborate. Laid back hospitality lowers the barriers for me and, I believe, makes it easier for my friend knowing they can come and I won't have to make special arrangements. If, however, they invite me for a meal, it will probably still be a bit lavish (and delicious!) but that's OK.

3) The mobile phone

This is an essential piece of kit! It's the main way today that friends keep in touch on the move. Younger people in the West 'get' this more easily than older ones like me, and they are right on the same wavelength as their Eastern counterparts. A Pakistani believer said that as a Muslim he used to have daily contact by mobile with the 17 members of his extended family, but after he turned to Christ they all dropped him. How lonely would that be when you are used to constantly sharing your news with family!

Keeping in touch like this is so much easier than it used to be. So, even if texting doesn't come naturally to you, learn to use it as a great way to show your friend that you are thinking of them during the day. Heed God's promptings, and if he prompts you to contact your friend (of Muslim background or any background) then just send them a quick SMS or WhatsApp. It might just make all the difference to them.

Your mobile is also the best way to remind your friend about appointments. In the West, an event in the diary is assumed to be confirmed, even weeks beforehand, with no further reminder needed. But you can't assume that in many Eastern cultures, nor indeed in the increasingly spontaneous culture of younger Westerners. An appointment is only provisional until you confirm it, maybe a day or two beforehand. Some individuals even need a repeat reminder an hour or two beforehand! A phone call or text is also more personal than a diary; it shows your friend that you really do hope they will come along. If they don't turn up then don't be afraid to ask them about it afterwards. They need to know that it matters to you and you missed them.

Finally the mobile phone is your friend's gateway to the internet, where they can find all kinds of teaching and worship including in their mother tongue. Will the smartphone be the discipleship tool of the 21st century? Well, the place of people in discipling will never be dislodged by technology since it's disciples who make disciples. But as a discipling tool, phones will take over more and more from books. In Chapter 7 we'll talk more about these opportunities.

---

17 Romans 12:13, NIV.

4) Explain how church works

Imagine for a moment that you as a Westerner have just become a Muslim and you have come along to the mosque. You meet a sea of strangers and struggle with an unfamiliar liturgy. You feel out of place and you don't want to do the wrong thing. What would help you most in that situation? I guess you most need a person to meet you outside beforehand, take you in and show you where to sit, stay with you there to guide you through the prayer rituals, and introduce you to their friends afterwards.

Now turn that scenario round. The way a mosque works feels alien to you, while church is comfortable and familiar. But to your friend, who spent all their previous life as a Muslim, mosque is familiar and church is strange. So what would help them most? Clearly, it's you they need most. They need you to meet up with them beforehand, sit with them in church, explain what's going on, show them what to do and where to find the Bible passages, and afterwards introduce them to other people.

Especially if your friend is new to your church, this could really help them. Later they won't need it so much. Meanwhile, however, some deeper questions might start kicking in.

Questions like these:

- Is 'going to church' simply equivalent to 'going to the mosque'?
- Why are there so many denominations, all with different customs?
- Must I leave my own culture at the door when I step into church?
- Should I join a white Western church or one which is closer to my background culture?
- What does it mean in practice to belong to this new community?

Don't assume that the church where a Muslim first comes to Christ, or even the church which baptised them, is the one where they will settle long-term. No one church 'possesses' them. It is their right to make their own choice. Different sizes and styles of churches suit different individuals and their needs can change over time. But if your friend seeks your advice on choosing a church, points to look out for might include:

- The church intentionally makes visitors welcome (including at coffee time);
- Its helps believers grow in understanding and obeying the Bible;
- The home groups give proper pastoral support;
- It helps members grow in using their gifts for service;
- It has an ethnic mix;
- Your friend easily reach there if they don't have a car.

5) Expand their circle of Christian friends

It's wonderful to have a close friend of Muslim background, but it's not healthy to make this an exclusive friendship. At some point something might cause the relationship to cool, and then they will need others. Also, you have certain gifts to help your friend but other Christians have gifts you lack. So look for ways to introduce your friend to other believers. That can start during the coffee time after the service, and then you could introduce your friend into a home group. Joining you on your church weekend away could be a great opportunity for them to be part of Christ's body on a deeper level. Take informal opportunities too to introduce your friend to others in your circle: family occasions, for instance, or when your friends are hanging out together.

Your friend should also get to know Christ's followers from other churches and other backgrounds, especially those of Muslim background. Often former Muslims suppose that "I'm the only person from my country/ethnic group who has ever turned to Christ". But these days that's not the case. For instance, in Britain there are Muslim background believers who are Arabs, Afghans, Bangladeshis, Iranians, Kurds, Nigerians, Pakistanis, Somalis and Turks - just for starters! Some of these groups have just a handful of believers in Britain, while for others it is hundreds, and for Iranians thousands. When BMBs can meet each other and realise that they aren't alone, that they aren't oddities but there are many others who have made the same choice as them to follow Jesus, it has an incredible impact. "So I'm part of an *ummah*[18] which is not just white and western but includes people like me!" This is important for helping them join the dots in their identity.

However, since these believers of Muslim background are spread across different churches in different cities, they may never get to meet each other until they are introduced. There are different ways to connect them. One way is by personally introducing them to each other on a 1:1 basis, while checking with the second believer that they are happy to be introduced. Another way is to let your friend know about gatherings or conferences of former Muslims following Jesus (see joiningthefamily.org for more details).

A third way is for you and your Christian friends to organise a one-time event where you invite all the believers of Muslim background you know about in your district. My wife and I first tried this a few years ago in Oxford and it was an amazing experience. We invited all the Muslim background believers we knew in the area and found others through local churches. About twenty of them came and filled our home with chatter and joy as they made connections and found so much in common. We shared food and fellowship and got to know each other and most stayed late into the evening. That became an annual event, and a highlight of our year.

However, don't take it for granted that former Muslims will always be keen to meet each other. They may be more cautious about it than you expect. This is especially true in Muslim majority countries where they can run into real difficulties if betrayed by an infiltrator to the group, as I have seen from experience. Even in the West, they don't always want to have contact with other Christians of their

---

18 An Arabic word often used by Muslims of their global community, and sometimes by BMBs for the community of Christ's followers worldwide.

background, especially at the beginning of their faith journey. This may be due to security, especially if they are British born from a settled Muslim community (e.g., Pakistani or Somali), where gossip about them can spread rapidly through the community and may cause hostility. Or perhaps for a time they want to cut themselves off from totally their old culture in order to establish their new Christian identity. This isn't necessarily their long term position but it can be a stage on the identity journey.

So, take each person as an individual and respect their wishes. If they are keen to meet another believer of Muslim background that's great. If they are not yet ready, there are usually reasons which may not be obvious. It's important to give your friend space and not pressurise them to meet other believers of Muslim background until they are ready. But in due course they will gain a great deal if they can overcome the trust barrier and connect with others of their own background.

Be there when it hurts

I regret the times when I failed to notice that my friends of Muslim background were fragile. I found out about it later and I wish I had been a better support at the time. Now I am starting to recognise some patterns of when they may be vulnerable and this helps me to be more aware next time. Here are some of those patterns.

1) Missing out on Muslim family occasions

Family is so important in Muslim cultures, that it is hard to imagine life without them! The year is punctuated by special occasions when Muslim families are together:

- the two annual Eids when everyone dresses in their finest and visits each other;
- weddings and funerals when all the relatives gather from far and wide;
- births of nephews, nieces, cousins;
- night-time feasting in Ramadan following the day-time fast.

Therefore to be frozen out of such events is deeply painful. Bilquis Sheikh felt wounded by the "calculated exclusion from great moments in the family", and the "painful boycott" when left out of a family funeral.[19] Mourning in many Muslim cultures is very public, while in Britain it is quite private. People feel awkward knowing how to comfort a bereaved person and may even avoid the topic altogether or just stick a card through the door. Please don't do this with your friend of Muslim background. Ask them how their relative died and allow them to externalise their sorrow.

My friend Karim used to be a Muslim *imam* in East Africa. One Friday in the

19 Bilquis Sheikh, *I Dared to Call Him Father*, (Kingsway, 1978), p.89-93.

mosque, after preaching the weekly sermon, when he heard a voice so loud that it cracked the windows, "I am Jesus, follow me!" He obeyed that voice that very day and became Christ's follower. (You can hear more of his remarkable story in the *Friendship First* DVD course). Now he lives in Britain and I was there on his wedding day when he married a lovely British Christian. He is so grateful for her, yet that happy day was also tinged with sadness for him:

Karim (former imam)

I miss my Muslim family many times, some times are harder than others. When I talk about this, I have a heavy heart. The worst moment was when I got married. I had been to many weddings and seen people who have their family, relatives, their friends and everyone come, and here was I getting married without a single member of my family on my wedding day! And I woke up in the morning and I just burst into tears. I didn't even want to go to my wedding anymore as I just felt like "Oh, why God have you punished me to let me be in this situation?"[20]

Can you imagine bursting into tears on your wedding day? And do you understand why it was so hard for Karim. Do you understand it with your mind, and feel it in your heart too? Another vulnerable time for Karim each year is the Muslim fasting month of Ramadan:

Ramadan is a family occasion, you normally have fellowship with your family; you are there with them, you do things together, you are part of the whole family. Now for me during Ramadan, I am left isolated. My Christian friends don't know about Ramadan much, so some of them don't even know that Muslims have started fasting. And my Muslim friends don't regard me as part of them, so I am left isolated in my little corner in my place in a room somewhere.[21]

So any occasion when your friend would normally be present at a Muslim family event, but is now excluded, is bound to be a hard time. Like other forms of loss and grief, working through it is a process and sometimes they will feel stronger than at other times. We need to be aware of these vulnerable times to sit with our BMB friends and listen to them. However, in some Muslim families the rejection is less severe, and even in difficult situations the damaged bridges may be repaired over time (see Chapter 9).

2) Missing out on Christian family occasions

Believers of Muslim background feel vulnerable not only when excluded from Muslim family occasions but also when they miss out on Christian family

---

20 *Joining the Family* course.
21 *Joining the Family* course.

occasions. The worst of these is Christmas, as several BMBs have told me. If church members are all busy celebrating Christmas with their own relatives, then where will the Muslim-background believers turn, whose relatives don't celebrate Christmas? Will they just go to church on Christmas morning and then wander back alone to their room while everyone else tucks into a feast? It's not that we deliberately *exclude* these spiritual relatives at Christmas, it's that we forget to *include* them. It's then that our concept of church as family really breaks down. Of course, this is not just about BMBs but anyone without a family at Christmas.

Consider inviting your friend to celebrate Christmas with you, ideally on Christmas Day itself. Some British families are used to having non-family joining in for Christmas lunch and spending the day with them. But other families find that harder and you may be obliged to fit in with your blood relatives. In such a case, you could do something with your friend to mark Christmas on a nearby day, but also try to find someone else who could invite your friend over on Christmas Day itself even if they don't see much of them the rest of the year.

What about holidays? If circumstances allow, can you invite along your friend of Muslim background to join you and your group on holiday? That could be a holiday for singles or a family holiday, church holiday week, or a Christian camp you are helping at. It's a great opportunity for getting on a deeper level with your friend and showing you really count them as family.

3) Times of illness

A third time when your friend will feel especially vulnerable is when they are ill, with no one to take care of them. Fyaz was in that situation when he told me on the phone, "If I was with my blood family they would look after me, but I have no one".[22]

So if your friend is on their own, be aware of that. Of course, that's not unique to those of Muslim background, since very many people do live on their own in our country. Looking out for them is part of what we should do for anyone in that situation. But it doesn't always come naturally until we realise it. Maybe 'being family' for those of Muslim background will help us be more alert to 'being family' generally.

Is God calling you to this?

In this chapter we have started learning how we can care for our individual friend of Muslim background. A comprehensive list of 'do's' and 'don'ts' isn't possible and isn't necessary. Instead, make a start with the guidelines in this chapter, keep an open heart for your friend, and pick up the rest as you go along. We repeat again: you don't need to be an expert:

22 Personal communication.

Horst Pietzsch (experienced mentor)

As brothers or sisters in Christ our purpose is to walk alongside a MBB[23]. It is not so much about right answers or knowledge. It is more about walking the road together, praying, encouraging, having fellowship, correcting, discipling, tutoring and waiting on God's answer to prayer. In other words, just being a true sister or brother in the Lord. The MBB needs to see Christ in you and to observe how to lead a Christian life.[24]

How do you know if the Lord is calling you to be 'close family' to a believer of Muslim background? Most likely it will happen if God brings such a person into your life and asks you to love them. If he does that, go with the flow and see where it leads. If he doesn't then don't worry about it. As you pray he can guide you. The main thing is just to be available for the Lord to use if he wants. You can't calculate it beforehand. Step in the shallows first and let God decide how deep to take you.

POINTS TO PONDER:

1 Jesus Christ promised that those who have left home, family or property for his sake will receive them many times over in this life, along with persecutions. How can we, the church, be the practical fulfilment of this promise? Think of examples from Favour's story.

2 How do you feel about the idea of being 'close family' to a believer of Muslim background? Does it seem a privilege or an intimidating responsibility? Bring your feelings to God.

3 In the section 'A heart of love – what is involved?' we made five practical suggestions. If you have a BMB friend, ask them which of these five would encourage them, or if anything else would be helpful.

4 Christ's followers of Muslim background are growing in number. Maybe there are several in your district, but how can you find out?

---

23 'Muslim Background Believer', meaning the same as 'Believer of Muslim Background'.
24 Horst Pietzsch, *Welcome Home: Caring for converts from a Muslim background*, (SIM, 2010), p.11.

Joining the Family

CHAPTER SIX

Going deeper in the friendship

(Tim writing...)

In the last chapter, Jan said that 'a heart of love' is the greatest quality needed to be a friend for Christ's follower of Muslim background. "It can be incredibly time-consuming to be supporting somebody who is exploring and discovering faith in Jesus", she continues. "They need somebody to be on the end of a phone, and you need to be available to see them two or three or four times a week if necessary, and phone them every day."[1]

This intense involvement won't be forever or for everyone, but for some it may be needed, and this chapter is for those situations. We consider practical, emotional and financial aspects, and also the nature of the relationship itself which rightly evolves over time.

Helping in practical ways

Javed grew up in an Afghan Muslim family and became Christ's follower in Britain. These days he is active in ministry among Afghan people. He has chosen to live on a reduced income in order to free up more time for this ministry:

Javed (Afghan Christian leader)

When you are involved with people's lives it's not easy just to say "God bless you" and just leave them. At times I receive phone calls from them even in the middle of night; when they're facing any problems I have tried to attend to whatever problems they've got.[2]

---

1   *Joining the Family* course.
2   *Joining the Family* course.

If we care for our friend spiritually, we can't avoid being involved practically. "We know what real love is because Jesus gave up his life for us. So we also ought to give up our lives for our brothers and sisters".[3] Let's think about the practical areas of accommodation, work and financial help.

1) Accommodation

Do you remember in Chapter 3 how Nigel the vicar described a BMB asylum seeker who turned up at his vicarage with no home and almost no possessions? Nigel took the man into his home and, along with the church members, helped him start to build a new life. (In Chapter 11 we explore in more depth the issue of asylum.) Sometimes believers need accommodation just for a few nights in a crisis or when they arrive in a new city. If it's a longer term need, then take it a step at a time, starting with an initial agreed period and deciding later whether to extend it and whether they should make a financial contribution.

2) Work

Generally, if the person is able to find work it's a good thing. It gives them self-respect, keeps them busy, and (for new immigrants) helps them to gain confidence in the host country and learn its language. It also gives them a wider circle of acquaintances and an opportunity to live for Christ in a non-Christian setting.

But how to set about finding a job? Usually something can be found, and even poorly paid work is a stepping-stone to a better job later. But my friend Ali had to overcome two hurdles for this. First was his cultural expectation. He came from an upper-class family in his home country which viewed any kind of menial work as dishonourable. I had to learn why this mattered to him and to make allowances for it. He needed to grasp (which he did over time) that even manual work is honourable when done for God.

Ali's second challenge was the practical one of how to actually find employment. He found it very discouraging to keep applying for jobs and being turned down. I and another friend then put effort into helping him find something. The very fact that we were alongside him encouraged him a lot. In the end we helped him find a part-time job on low pay; but it was better than nothing! He flourished, grew in confidence and skills, learned punctuality and had an identity. Before long, he found a better full-time job which even came with a company car.

3) Loans and gifts

Should we help our friend financially if they ask for it? This is a sensitive issue in any situation and all the more so when there are different cultural expectations. Western culture stresses independence: you stand on your own feet, you go it alone, you don't ask others for help, and anyway if help is needed you turn to the government or an institution. Meanwhile, those who give financially do so through charities, not to individuals. By contrast, in many Muslim cultures charity

---

3   1 John 3:16, NLT.

is more personal and people are more interdependent. If you are in trouble the government won't help you, so you depend on your circle of family and friends. Those who are better off are obliged to help their poorer relatives, and they do this person-to-person not through a charity. This personalised safety net has some advantages but it also creates a power imbalance between the giver as 'patron' and the receiver who is dependent.

Such generalisations don't always apply, but they help us understand why, when a new believer is told "Welcome to the family", they may have the cultural expectation of family providing financial help when needed. They may expect their spiritual mentor to be their financial patron too, whereas western Christians would draw a clear dividing line between these.

Therefore, what will you do if your friend asks you for a loan? I have had this experience many times. I respond in different ways on different occasions. Sometimes I have loaned money at particular times of need. For instance, one friend badly needed money as advance rent for a month. He was just starting a job so would be able to repay later. Several months later I had heard nothing and was wondering whether to mention it or not. But one day he handed over the whole amount (several hundred pounds) in cash; in this case it was good for our relationship and for his self-respect that I had made him a loan, not a gift.

On other occasions I knew the person's need was genuine, short-term and could not be repaid, and I have helped as a gift. If it was an ongoing need I have sometimes looked for other Christians to help too (respecting confidentiality), to spread the load and to somewhat reduce the personalised dependency syndrome.

Several times I have lent money which wasn't repaid. In such cases I didn't mind the financial loss so much as the loss of relationship, when my friend got embarrassed about it and started avoiding me. Then again, others seem to continue as friends without embarrassment and I don't know whether to mention the unpaid loan to them. So it's not easy to know what to do and I sometimes make mistakes. However, I have known believers to be greatly blessed by the help they received (like Favour in Chapter 5), and others who were deeply discouraged when their Christian brothers and sisters failed to help. So if in doubt I prefer to be too open-handed than too tight-fisted. Yet boundaries are also important and we discuss that more below.

Helping your friend through emotional pain

Some BMBs are doing fine financially. I think of an Iranian couple who own a home and two small businesses, and their children study at a private school. Despite all this, their marriage was in bad shape and the wife was about to kill herself at the point that Jesus met her unexpectedly early one morning (in person, at her workplace). He turned her life around, then her husband's. That couple have never needed financial help, rather they are in a position to help others. But they have certainly needed lots of biblical teaching, spiritual guidance and emotional support. Emotional pain is very likely to be there for your friend, even if it's not obvious at first. For nearly every BMB I know, the deepest pain relates to their Muslim family, as Roxy explains...

(Roxy writing...)

Believers of Muslim background have had varied experiences of family and community life: some of these are very loving and positive experiences, while some are filled with varying degrees of control and oppression, even physical violence and abuse. When people from Muslim backgrounds share their stories we sometimes assume they must have had a very difficult life in their birth family. This may be the case for some, but not all and not the majority. Growing up many will have had a very happy, stable and loving home and family, where they felt accepted and were able to thrive as children.

This is reflected by Nabeel Qureshi's dedication to his parents in his excellent book *Seeking Allah, Finding Jesus* where he writes this to his mum ('Ammi') and dad ('Abba'):

> ### Nabeel Qureshi (who grew up in the UK and USA)
> This book is dedicated to my parents. Ammi and Abba, your undying love for me even when you feel I have sinned against you, is second only to God's love for His children. I pray you will one day realize His love is truly unconditional, that he has offered forgiveness to us all. On that day, I pray that you would accept His redemption, so we might be a family once again. I love you with all my heart.[4]

For people like Nabeel, their family life may not have been perfect but it was positive. Therefore, when they come to faith in Jesus, the emotions around their conversion can be quite confusing and difficult to deal with. Here Nabeel describes the crushing agony he felt after telling his beloved parents that he must follow Jesus at all costs:

> I was a crumpled heap on the ground, trembling before God (...) The night before, I had looked into Abba's eyes as they welled with tears. Those eyes that had so tenderly cared from me since he whispered the adhan (call to prayer) into my ears. The eyes that softly closed in prayer every night as he invoked the protection of God (...) To be the cause of the only tears I had seen those eyes shed, I could not bear it.
>
> "Why, God...?"
>
> Though Abba did not say much, what he did say has haunted me ever

---

4   Nabeel Qureshi, *Seeking Allah, Finding Jesus*, (Zondervan 2014), p.7.

since. The man who stood tallest in my life, my archetype of strength, my father, spoke these words through palpable pain: "Nabeel, this day, I feel as if my backbone has been ripped out from inside me". The words tore through me. It felt like patricide. I had not given up just my life to follow Jesus, I was killing my father. [5]

He has never stood as tall since that day. I extinguished his pride.

Nabeel's relationship with his parents survived but the long-term pain continued for him and them:

After recovering from the initial shock, my parents made two things very clear about their stance toward me: they felt utterly betrayed, yet they loved me regardless. Emotions raged, harsh words were spoken, and arguments flared, but they did not ostracize me. On the one hand, this was a blessing because I remained a part of my family. On the other hand, it was extremely painful because I had to weather emotional storms regularly. Ammi cried every time I saw her for almost the next two years, often while painfully indicting me for destroying our family's joy.[6]

When a believer of Muslim background discovers the love of Jesus he or she feels excited and happy, but there is also a sense of guilt and the shame of leaving the family's faith and becoming an 'Apostate'. This "confusing and emotionally draining state", writes Turkish BMB Ziya Meral, brings a strong sense of shame "due to the social pressure that labels them as enemies and betrayers".[7] They may go through a period of denying these more difficult feelings as they may feel that they should only feel excited by their new-found faith. Their Christian friends may not know these feelings are there.

After coming to faith BMBs may experience a roller coaster of emotions, some of which are very difficult to make sense of, such as the joy and exhilaration of new experiences of the Holy Spirit and the freedom to pray in a language they understand, or the sense of sadness that they are the only member of their family who made the decision to become a follower of Jesus.

For many of us, life is lived alongside those who love and accept us, but if, as is the case for many BMBs, they no longer have those people there, they will grieve that loss. This could involve a journey through from sadness, denial, and anger to acceptance and letting go of the lost relationships. This journey can take months or years. The individual in the journey needs help to process and understand their feelings.

---

5   Nabeel Qureshi, *Seeking Allah, Finding Jesus*, p.280.
6   Nabeel Qureshi, *Seeking Allah, Finding Jesus*, p.280, 286.
7   Ziya Meral, 'Conversion and Apostasy: A Sociological Perspective', *Evangelical Missions Quarterly* Vol.42, 2006, p.508-513.

For other BMBs there is more difficult emotional damage, done to them by their experiences as children and because of the rejection and persecution of their Muslim family and community. This needs God's healing at a deep level. It takes courage to face and they cannot find this without the support and care of wise friends around them, as we described for Hannah in Chapter 4. Some of the emotions your friend may express can seem shocking to us, but it is important we don't add to those feelings of guilt and shame by displaying shock. If we feel unable to hear about these things it's important we are honest and help them to find alternative appropriate support.

Fyaz (British born Pakistani)

My family know I'm a Christian now and they just don't want anything to do with me. They regard me as a deserter, and they don't see me. My parents had another child when I left home who is now in his twenties. I have never seen him, I've never met him. I've got nieces, I've got nephews, and they have been cheated out of an uncle, I have been cheated out of a family. So it's hard, and when you go through tribulations, you are quick to think about your family at that point. Now, I don't see them.

My mum is the main cause of the problems at home. I hated her with a passion, a passion that could have escalated to murder. I would like to physically tell her that I forgive her, and to hug her. And to tell her that I don't hate her. I don't hate her any more. That's what I would want to do, to exercise the love of Christ to her. [8]

Five things we can do to help

- **Listen to your friend**, and show compassion in seeking to understand their situation: don't just assume what they feel but ask, and allow them to be honest. Share your own experiences of dealing with difficult emotions. Be happy with those who are happy, and weep with those who weep. (Romans 12:15)

- **Pray with and for your friend**, not as judgement of their past but as blessing and hope, peace and comfort. Ask them if it's OK before you do pray for them, bearing in mind that someone who trusted you enough to share experiences and emotions with you is in a vulnerable position. They need you to respect them and care for them. I have had helpful experiences where people prayed with me and I felt hopeful and comforted but I have also received prayer from people who assumed that the problem was demonic; they began to pray it out of me, at which point I ran from

---

8 *Joining the Family* course.

them very quickly and never returned there for prayer.

- **Refer your friend to outside help** if appropriate and needed, e.g. counsellors, retreat and healing centres. Remember you can't do it all and there are some things that only those properly trained can help with. You don't want to cause more damage.

- **Remember that healing can take time** and this may be a process that needs to happen for them. Often God does more beneath the surface than we realise.

- Lastly and most importantly, **love lived out** is a healing thing in itself, as 1 Corinthians 13 reminds us:
  Love is patient, love is kind. It does not envy, it is not proud. It does not dishonour others, it is not self seeking, it is not easily angered, it keeps no record of wrongs. Love does not delight in evil but rejoices with the truth. It always protects, always trusts, always hopes, always perseveres. Love never fails.[9]

A respectful but honest friendship

(Tim writing...)

1) Being respectful

First and foremost, you and your friend of Muslim background are equals. You are equal as friends, and you both have much to learn from your give-and-take relationship. And you are equal in God's sight: fallen human beings with faults and cultural blind-spots, but also his precious children.

And yet, if your friend is a new believer, there's also an inherent imbalance in the relationship because you have walked further than them on the Christian path. You know your way round the Bible better and Christ has been working for longer on your character, so the person looks to you as a mentor. There may also be an imbalance in age, wealth or influence especially if, for instance, your friend is an international student or asylum seeker.

That imbalance is not a problem in itself, for we in turn have older Christians we look up to. We all need mentors and role models, as we will see in Chapter 7. But let's just be sensitive to this power dynamic because it could subtly affect things if, for instance, you have strong advice to give your friend, or they expect strong advice from you. Depending on your friend's cultural background (which varies), they might expect their mentor to tell them what to do or even make their decisions for them. That's potentially dangerous, for your friend is actually

---

9   1 Corinthians 13: 4-8a, NIV.

not your follower but Christ's follower. Your job is to help them follow Christ's guidance. But then, part of Christ's guidance will come to them through you. So we need to strike a balance between giving too much advice and too little.

Personally I find it hard to strike that balance. Sometimes I have held back from giving guidance when I should have done. Other times I have given advice too strongly; even if my words themselves were not so strong, the hidden message was that I would think better of the person if they followed my advice, and my influence over them may have made it hard for them to resist. I recall a particular occasion when I suggested to a believer that she take in our mutual friend as a housemate. I thought it was just a suggestion, but she took it as strong advice, and went ahead even though her heart wasn't in it. Later their relationship turned sour and I had to apologise for the part I had inadvertently played in this.

Another area where respect is vital is confidentiality. If your friend tells you something personal and private, you have no right to pass it on to another person without permission – not even as a prayer request! And if you're not sure whether your friend sees it as a strict secret, then just ask them.

To summarise, the relationship with our friend of Muslim heritage must be respectful. He or she is an adult. They can and should make their own decisions, and though we gladly give advice we also make it clear that "I may be wrong on this, and you need to seek God yourself". We avoid their getting into permanent dependency on us, and even if it starts as a relationship of unequal power, we look for it to evolve into a friendship of equals.

2) Being honest

Sometimes a BMB friend has let me down repeatedly and I struggle to know what to do. Should I confront them on this? If so, how to do it appropriately? I find it so hard to get this right. Often I hang back from confrontation, thinking "I'll go the second mile for now and bring this up later at a better time". I don't mind going that second mile, or the third or fourth. But eventually it affects my relationship with my friend and how I feel towards them. More important is their relationship with the Lord. If they are repeatedly doing something which impedes their spiritual growth, should I keep quiet and let him convict them by his Spirit in his own way at the right time? Or does God want to speak to them through my saying something?

I don't have a magic answer for this. But here are a few things I have learned over the years about how to confront my friend in a gentle, humble way:

- **Put credit in the 'relationship bank' first.** A warm, strong friendship makes it easier for me to give occasional critique and for my friend to accept it. It gives me the right to speak.

- **Choose the right time and place.** I should never confront my friend in front of others, and never when in a hurry, and preferably when I'm not tired. If in doubt, I don't blurt it out but wait and pray some more.

- **Get my emotions right with the Lord.** If I don't empty out my anger, disappointment or frustration before the conversation, it will definitely spill out during it.

- **Sandwich any criticism between two layers of affirmation.** This provides a secure context for the critique.

- **Emphasise that I'm not perfect either.** I too disappoint my friend at times, and I don't claim to be better than him. We both let each other down. But we can be honest with each other simply because we are such good friends.

3) Resolving conflict

Spending many years in Pakistan, I found that the concepts of 'please', 'thank you' and 'sorry' do exist but are not directly stated as often as in Britain. Indeed, some Pakistanis think I use these phrases too often! So there's a cultural difference. My Pakistani friends won't thank me very profusely or write a thank-you card after coming for a meal, and I have learned not to expect it. But they will probably show it in a different way, such as an expensive gift, which in my culture is embarrassing but in theirs is the appropriate way. However Roxy, with Pakistani parentage, but relating to British people, found that:

> **Roxy**
> I hadn't realised I never apologised in the words "I'm sorry" until someone pointed it out. I might show it in different ways but not say the words; and the same with "please" and "thank you". Someone said, "You are obviously grateful but you don't put it in words". I felt embarrassed and ashamed that I had never realised. Praise God that someone had the courage to confront me for this.[10]

Moreover, different cultures resolve conflict in different ways. As a British person, if I have an issue with someone I want to talk straight with them to sort it out. But in Pakistan I discovered that this approach made people uncomfortable, and even offended them. Their way to handle conflict was less direct, which I learned to understand. But it still saddened me whenever their conflict-avoidance meant they just stopped talking, leading to years of bitter alienation. Roxy agrees that in that culture "confrontation is quite difficult and it leads to avoidance which becomes a big issue in relationships".[11] Additionally,

---

10 Personal conversation.
11 Personal conversation.

in Pakistan and other hierarchical cultures, in a situation of conflict the person more junior in the pecking order (young, female or poor) is typically made to surrender to the senior one without ever being allowed to address the issue. This buys temporary peace but not a lasting solution.

This cultural baggage of failing to resolve conflicts well has caused endless damage to newly emerging fellowships of Christ's followers – in Muslim countries and in the West. So much so, that someone did their whole PhD on the subject of disharmony in Iranian fellowships in the West.[12] I find it tragic when believers start to meet, then they fall out over something, and they don't have the mechanisms to move forward, so the fellowship breaks up in hurt and disarray. That's why I included a whole chapter on 'Solving our Disputes' in the discipleship course *Come Follow Me* (see Appendix 1). You might like to study that topic with your friend. Both of you can do this as co-learners, for your friend can help you see your own cultural blind spots in this area.

However, reconciliation cannot just be taught in theory, it must also be demonstrated in flesh and blood. How can I show my friend a godly way to apologise and ask for forgiveness? Only by modelling it myself. We can't avoid being a role model, as we shall see in Chapter 7. So let's learn to be transparent with our friend, quick to apologise, and honest about our failures and our relationship struggles. Fafar, as a new believer, was deeply impacted when she saw these qualities in her Christian friend who had been hurt by someone else:

Fafar (Iranian BMB)

I was aware of the hurt she had suffered and she was actually acting her faith by forgiving, and praying, and still having a friendship with this person, and it was very important to see this demonstrated in the life of a Christian person, someone who truly obeyed Christ.[13]

In summary, appropriate confrontation isn't easy. I find it hard to get the balance between challenging my BMB friend too much, and not doing it enough. But despite my many failures in this area, sometimes it has worked out well. Ali told me he is grateful for the times I and others have challenged him, knowing that we did so out of love. "Faithful are the wounds of a friend".[14]

4) Having boundaries

Here too, different cultures have different expectations. If you are a Westerner, your friendship with a believer of Muslim background is a cross-cultural one, so it helps to understand each other's assumptions. In general, individualistic cultures (such as white middle class British) like clear boundaries: "my house,

---

12 Roy Oksnevad, 'An Investigation into the Components of Disharmony in Iranian Muslim Background Churches in the Diaspora' (PhD dissertation, Trinity International University, 2013).
13 *Friendship First* DVD course.
14 Proverbs 27:6. NIV.

my money, my personal space, my time for family". By contrast many collectivist cultures have a more blurred attitude to boundaries, so that people share a lot more in terms of space, time and property. Taken across the whole world, blurred-boundary people probably outnumber strict-boundary people. So clear boundaries are not in themselves 'better', and indeed the Bible might challenge our Western culture to share more than we do.

However, it's also true that your friend is living in a Western environment and needs to adjust to this, as well as recognising how it affects your outlook. Maybe your friend could respect your boundaries more for your sake, and you could loosen yours up for their sake. Once your friendship is well established, you might like to discuss these things with each other. They affect, for example, the different notions of 'making appointments' that we discussed in the last chapter.

5) An evolving relationship

Recall how, in the book of Acts, the apostle Paul was still quite a new believer when he tried to join up with the Jerusalem Christians. But, fearing he was a spy, they kept him at arm's length. It took Barnabas, nicknamed 'son of encouragement', to take the risk of befriending Paul and introducing him to the church leaders. Barnabas was a good friend to Paul, and his mentor at this early stage. Several years later Barnabas again was a mentor to Paul, training him in ministry in the church at Antioch, though by this stage they were also colleagues. When that church sent them out as fellow missionaries, Barnabas was still at first the senior partner, but before long Paul had overtaken him as the most prominent leader. We trace this evolving relationship in Acts chapters 9 to 13. What I love about Barnabas is the gracious way he was willing to let Paul keep growing into ministry, leadership and prominence.

Much of what I have written in Chapters 5 and 6 assumes that your BMB friend is fairly new in the faith, and that your role is to encourage and mentor them as Barnabas did for Paul. That is fine in the early stages, but it should not stay that way long-term, any more than it did for those two leaders. As Horst Pietzsch writes, "In the beginning, we will give more attention to the MBBs" but over time "we have to give them space again".[15]

I have known Rasheeda since she was still a new Christian. It has been wonderful to see her grow in Christ over the years and develop in ministry. I echo her wise advice here and I take it as a reminder to myself:

Rasheeda, after nearly 10 years as Christ's follower

Those that care for believers of Muslim background need to evolve and change over time in their relationships with BMBs. Initially they need to mentor and guide and pray with the BMBs. However, as time progresses they need humility to learn from BMBs because they do have something important to share that only they can give the church.

---

15 Horst Pietzsch, Welcome Home: *Caring for converts from a Muslim background*, (SIM, 2010), p.11.

Keeping fresh in this ministry

Highs and lows

Looking back over nearly four decades of friendships with former Muslims following Jesus, it has felt like a roller coaster ride of ecstatic highs and stomach-churning lows. The highs come from seeing a Muslim put their faith in Jesus, blossom as his disciple, keep witnessing to their community and produce the fruit of Christian maturity. It's just so thrilling to see God at work in their lives - and through them, in the lives of others.

The lows come when a dear friend succumbs to the onslaught of Muslim family pressure, or to those old tempters the world, the flesh and the devil. Maybe they dropped out of Christian fellowship for whatever reason. Or maybe they married a Muslim person and got gradually reabsorbed into the Muslim community, though very few go back to Islam with any conviction. Sometimes when believers threaten to return to Islam it springs more from emotional frustration than doctrinal conviction. One friend was upset with his circumstances and angry with his Christian friends; and he was longing for the security of being home with his Muslim family and the familiar framework of his Muslim upbringing. That's what 'returning to Islam' was about for him, and his threat to do that was more a cry for help than anything else. It was a worrying phase. He didn't act on his threat, but he may have another wobble in future.

Whenever I see someone who started well in the long distance race of faith, faltering after several laps or stepping out of the race altogether, it hurts so much! It's now three years since my friend Farookh was in a crisis. I had attended his baptism, helped with his rent hassles, had him stay in my home for a while, wrestled in prayer for him, wept for him and assured my Christian friends he would pull through. So when he told me he had decided to stop being a Christian, it hurt so much. I realise there was a whole mix of reasons for his decision, but it still hurt. Why is this? It's partly because I had poured myself into him; and I heed the danger of treating him or anyone as 'my' project. But my hurt is also because Jesus poured himself out for Farookh, and continues to love him, and longs for him to return. And it's also because it honours Christ when his followers stay firm to the end and dishonours him when they don't.

Therefore we will experience some disappointments as we care for believers of Muslim background, as can happen with those of any background. So Yes, it does happen. But in my own experience, they are not so many as are sometimes claimed, *especially* if they are well cared for as new Christians. So it's a roller-coaster ride. Sometimes my heart bursts with joy and sometimes it bleeds. In my experience, the highs and lows come as a package. You can't have one without the other.

Digging deeper into God

Jan too has known the highs and lows of this ministry:

Jan

It can be very disappointing at times, people blow hot and cold. Many times with my friend who has come to Christ, I have arranged to meet with her and she calls off at the last minute. I have rearranged my whole afternoon and then she phones up five minutes beforehand and says she can't meet. And then other times she wants to meet very regularly. We have to be willing to be there even when we are let down ourselves. But again, if we go back to God and think about the many times we let him down, how can we withdraw our support when he never withdrew his support for us?[16]

"We have to go back to God", says Jan. It's about digging deeper into God to find extra resources of patience. We lean into him and let him restore our perspective. With his help and for his sake, we hang in there for our friend through thick and thin. If we don't keep praying for this person, who will?

Better together than alone

Each believer of Muslim background should have not one but several people who can play the part of 'close family' as we described earlier. They help that person in complementary ways and they can encourage each other as they go along, and support each other in prayer. That's better than leaving it all to one person. So in a church where Muslims are coming to faith, a few mature Christians can be set aside for the vital ministry of caring for them. It is a lot more time-consuming than may appear on paper, for it revolves around relationships not lots of meetings. And these mature Christians are already probably in demand for other roles in the church. So it helps if the church leaders specifically recognise these people for this ministry, and we discuss this further in Chapter 10.

To those who are called to this ministry, Horst Pietzsch gives this advice:

Horst Pietzsch (mentor)

We are involved with God's people when we are for MBBs. That is a rewarding ministry (...) We must not expect them to consult us during 'office-hours'. Once you decide to be involved in ministry to MBBs, be in it wholeheartedly. Commit yourself to make a difference in the life of a MBB for the Lord's sake. Reschedule your life and adjust your priorities to accommodate this ministry.

We must get involved with others and join or form a team for caring for MBBs. But before we get involved in this ministry, we need to prepare ourselves and ensure we work at a pace that we ourselves do not burn

---

16 *Joining the Family* course.

out (…) We cannot compartmentalize our feelings. It doesn't work. We also have emotions. It is okay to cry when we fail to help someone or when we have deep feelings after a difficult situation. It is good for our own survival.[17]

'Our joy and crown'?

Finally, let's remember what St. Paul felt about the Thessalonian believers: "What is our hope, our joy, or the crown in which we will glory in the presence of our Lord Jesus when he comes? Is it not you?"[18] Here is the privilege of this ministry, and here too is a danger. If by thinking of new believers (of any background, not just Muslim) as "our joy and crown" we are treating them as our own personal project, we are in trouble. This changes our relationship with them, by making them more a commodity than a genuine friend; it dishonours the Lord, by seeking to make people our disciples rather than his; and it displaces the centre of our hope from him to them. While it's still true that these dear brothers and sisters in Christ are "our joy and crown", the greater truth still is that "The joy of the Lord is your strength".[19] And that's the best way to stay fresh in this ministry.

POINTS TO PONDER:

1 In this chapter Tim has reflected on his own joys, struggles and motivations in his friendships with believers of Muslim background. Which points did he make which resonate with your own experience, and which do not?

2 Roxy opened up the pain which so many BMBs feel about their Muslim families. If appropriate, gently ask your own BMB friend to share with you about their family, if they wish.

3 If you don't yet know a brother or sister in Christ who grew up in Islam, find someone who does, and ask them about any points that puzzled you in this chapter.

---

17 Horst Pietzsch, *Welcome Home: Caring for converts from a Muslim background*, (SIM, 2010), p.12.
18 1 Thessalonians 2:19, NIV.
19 Nehemiah 8:10, NIV.

Joining the Family

CHAPTER SEVEN

Growing in Christ

(Tim writing...)

The first draft for this chapter was called 'Helping your friend grow in Christ' – but I changed that title. It sounded too much like a one-way process! It gave the impression that mature Christians as 'disciplers' have reached the top of the ladder and now are reaching down to help newer 'disciples' to climb that ladder too. Actually we are all on the ladder, we are all on the journey, and we all have a long way to go.

St. Paul had already been Christ's follower more than 25 years when he wrote these words:

> *I want to know Christ (...) becoming like him (...) Not that I have already obtained all this, or have already arrived at my goal, but I press on (...)Forgetting what is behind and straining toward what is ahead, I press on toward the goal to win the prize for which God has called me heavenward in Christ Jesus.*[1]

Even as a mature Christian Paul didn't think he had 'arrived'. Nevertheless he was still able to write "Imitate me as I imitate Christ".[2] This chapter is about seeking that balance: accepting our responsibility to encourage and guide those who are new in the faith, while also humbly walking beside them as fellow-believers who still have much to learn. I am a disciple of Christ, so is my friend of Muslim background, so we each encourage the other as together we press on in the long-distance road of discipleship. That journey will last our whole lives, and its end goal is to become like Jesus!

---

1 Philippians 3:10-14, NIV.
2 1 Corinthians 11:1, NIV.

'In Christ'

I love the phrase 'in Christ' and my friends of Muslim background love it too. They were 'in' Islam and they are now 'in' Christ: united with him, bonded to him, hidden in him. They have died and been raised with him, and their identity is wrapped up in his identity. Perhaps you don't use that language very much in your Christian tradition, but the Bible uses it a lot, especially Paul in his epistles. It is rich, strong terminology. Also, this phrase 'in Christ' sidesteps the question of how much cultural Christianity a former Muslim needs to adopt. Some change more of their culture, some less, but that's a side issue. The main point for them is to be 'found in Christ' and 'pressing on towards the goal'[3] as Paul wrote.

So how do Christ's followers of Muslim background grow strong in him? It happens in much the same way as for Christ's followers of any background, though slightly modified by culture. Probably the things that helped you grow will prove to be similar for your friend of Muslim background.

- **Stop and think.** What things have helped you grow in Christ, up till now? You might like to make a list of them right now.

What factors help BMBs grow strong in Christ?

Several research projects have set out to ask this very question, including Don Little's book based on interviews with many experienced mentors of Arab BMBs, and unpublished projects by others including Tom Walsh.[4] Allowing for the fact that each researcher created their own categories with their own terminology, their actual conclusions are very similar. My own research in Pakistan also confirms these main factors in spiritual growth. So let's examine them now, and also ask what is going on under the surface? How and why do each of these factors help so much?

1) An individual mentor

Chapters 5 and 6 were all about being a good friend. So what's different about being a mentor? Actually it can be both at the same time, as Khalida found:

> #### Khalida (British BMB of Pakistani descent)
> The thing that really helped me grow in Christ when I first became a Christian was the fact that somebody really invested their time for me to be discipled. I remember a young lady who spent weeks and weeks and weeks, just every single evening, practically if I wanted, going through a discipleship programme with me. I thoroughly enjoyed it, it was really simple and great to understand. And she was my friend too. She wasn't just somebody discipling me and going through a

---

3 Philippians 3:14 again, NIV.
4 See the list in Appendix 1, and Don Little, Effective Discipling in Muslim Communities: Scripture, History and Seasoned Practices, (IVP 2015).

programme with me, she really was a true friend. And I think that made all the difference.[5]

For Khalida, the friendship with her mentor was important in its own right, but also was a way to help her know God and to go through a discipleship course in a relational way. The friendship was genuine but also intentional. It's not a question of being either friend or mentor, but of both in combination.

Being a role model

Probably the biggest influence which a mentor-friend has in the life of a new believer is as a role model. Maybe you think "I can't be a role model, I'm not good enough for that". But whether you like it or not, that's what you already are! All the time, much more than we realise, we are giving out messages by our comments, our tone of voice, our attitudes, our reactions when things go wrong. Most of the time we are not even aware of being a role model. For instance, when we just invite our friend round for a meal, we are modelling Christian hospitality. How do we welcome them at the door? How do we give thanks for the food? How do we relate to our spouse (if we have one) during the evening? All of this speaks volumes to our friend.

One Afghan said:
When I asked for Bible study, I didn't want to study the book, I was studying the person who was discipling me.[6]

New believers have faith in the unseen Jesus but still can't see him physically on earth. So they want to know what following him actually looks like in real life. When Chris when he turned from Islam to Christ, he needed someone to show him how to live this new life. His advice to mentors is, "Be a role model for them. Spend a lot of time with them. Show them by doing it yourself".[7]

I find this an intimidating thought. Sometimes believers of Muslim background have told my wife and I that they learned a lot from our family life, and I think "if only you knew how often we mess up!" Yet as we are transparent and share our lives with these dear friends, somehow God uses that. We don't have to be perfect. We just have to be real.

Since we can't avoid being a role model, it's best just to embrace it and ask God to use it despite our weaknesses. Gordon Hickson speaks about his own relationship with a particular friend of Muslim background:

Gordon Hickson (coordinator of the Mahabba network)
There's got to be a sense of no facades, that you're walking life, you're

---

5   *Joining the Family* course.
6   Told to me by a friend who used to work in Afghanistan.
7   *Joining the Family* course.

doing life together. It's life-on-life discipleship, they're learning from you. With this particular person I had to be very transparent. I had to not always be on top, I had to share with him some of my struggles, some of my battles. He learnt more from watching my life and watching me walking through things than he did by me just teaching him.

It's not just what you say. They become what you are, they copy you as you are copying Christ. They are actually looking at you, learning from you. So, it is really important that you understand that dynamic. It's not about the material, it's about your life. More than anything else, it's about who you are. [8]

So being perfect isn't important. What matters most is to be available and genuine. In fact, the way we respond when things go wrong can speak more than when everything is going right. If I can forgive someone who hurts me, or apologise when I have hurt them, and my BMB friend can see how I do that and follow my example, it's worth a thousand sermons!

We have seen how powerful this transforming friendship is for the growth of new believers. But remember this is not a merely one way process. It works in both directions and both people are changed. I personally have learned so much about following Jesus from my close friends of Muslim heritage. I think of a wise, gracious BMB friend who is older than me. Over the last 27 years, I have learned so much from him! Yes, it's true that we are responsible for being a role model to other believers. But it's also true that they and we together are disciples, walking along together in Jesus' footsteps, like those first disciples on the dusty roads of Palestine.

2) The community of Christ's followers

There are several reasons why this community needs to be real outside of just Sunday services. Firstly, identity is formed and forged in community. Following our rebirth in Christ, our identity is forged anew in a new community and we learn who we are in relation to those around us. The new community becomes what sociologists have called a "laboratory of transformation",[9] where adult converts see new possibilities for doing life differently from how they were reared as children.

Secondly, Christ's community gives affirmation to the new BMB that they really did make the right choice in choosing to follow him. Remember, their old community constantly gives them the message, "You are a fool and a traitor. You betrayed your family, you brought shame on us all and you have taken a crazy decision. But it's still not too late. Come back to Islam!" Faced with such a

---

8   *Joining the Family* course.
9   Peter Berger and Thomas Luckmann, *The Social Construction of Reality: A Treatise in the Sociology of Knowledge*, (Doubleday 1966), p.144.

barrage, who would not start, occasionally, to doubt themselves? In this mental tug-of-war, when one side is saying "You made the wrong decision", the new community needs to pull hard on the other side, assuring the person that "You made the right decision to follow Jesus!"

Thirdly, no one is called to be Christ's disciple on their lonely own. I was so sad when one BMB chose 'sheepalone@xxx' for his email address. Sheep alone are comfortless, directionless and vulnerable. We weren't designed to live the Christian life that way! When Jesus called the first disciples, he called them individually but also to join a close-knit group. As their numbers grew after Pentecost, still they remained deeply committed to each other, they "broke bread in their homes and ate together with glad and sincere hearts".[10] I have known some believers of Muslim background who tried to thrive on their own spiritually, without regular fellowship. It didn't work.

Fourthly, community in the form of a small group provides someone a safe space to open up and discuss the things they have been learning as Christ's follower. This includes the puzzling aspects and the setbacks. For a believer of Muslim background there are some benefits of this small group experience being with others like them, and some benefits in mixed-culture groups. Thus Iranians and Afghans who belong to different local churches for Sunday worship might appreciate meeting together as a mid-week small group to share in their own Farsi language. The pastors of those different local churches may find this kind of dual belonging unconventional, but it can work well, especially if those pastors keep in good contact with each other.

One final reason why BMBs, like all of us, need Christ's community is that it's easier to worship with others than on one's own. Worship transfers our attention from ourselves to God. Beholding him and adoring him, in a mysterious way we start to become like him – in Christ. Last Sunday in my local church in Asia, singing with more than a thousand other believers of a different culture to my own, I was suddenly overcome with a powerful conviction that, "this is my identity, and these are my people". Immediately afterwards came the communion service, and as I received the bread and wine I was again impacted by the sense that, "I am in Christ, I am bonded to him". I probably would not have experienced these two heart-thrilling moments had I stayed on my own in my room. I needed that shared worship.

3) God's transforming Word

We all have a worldview. This is our unconscious set of assumptions, our core belief system. It's the basic mindset that determines how we see the world. Think of it like the lens inside your eye - you don't notice that it's there, but you can't see anything without looking through it. In other words, your worldview is made up of the things you believe but don't know you believe.

---

10 Acts 2:46, NIV.

Our worldview begins to be formed very early in life, through our 'significant others' – especially our family, and later our friends and peer group. By the time a person reaches adulthood their worldview is firmly in place. Muslims and Hindus and atheists all have that lens in their mind as adults, and the lenses are different in each case. How they see God is different and this affects how they interpret life's events. So if a Muslim has a car crash it's interpreted as the will of Allah, for a Hindu it might be payment for previous sins, while for the atheist it simply means that the brakes failed!

For those who turn to Christ in adult life, their whole way of thinking needs to change. They bring their old lens with them, and only gradually does this get reshaped till they perceive things differently. This is true for new believers of any background. For instance, if we came from a materialistic Western background, it takes a long time to reshape our 'old lens' assumptions like:

- "What's mine is mine - my own private property";
- "I have to be self-sufficient, for it's weakness to receive help";
- "My Facebook image defines my identity".

Likewise, a Muslim who turns to Christ will also bring his or her old mental habits - ways of seeing the world and ways of seeing God. For example, many (not all) Muslims assume that:

- "God is too far away to care about my little concerns";
- "God sent this illness to punish me";
- "If I tell God my doubts he will be angry with me";
- "It's better to tell a lie than to dishonour someone".

Deep-level discipleship

Reshaping the lenses takes a long time! It happens when God's transforming Word gets to work on our worldview. He reshapes our lens to see things his way. He changes the way we think. Therefore the Bible tells us, "Let God transform you into a new person by changing the way you think".[11] This process, though gradual, is as radical as taking out the old chip from our brain and putting in a new one. It changes our core outlook, which in turn slowly transforms our values, attitudes and behaviour. This is deep level discipleship.

Take revenge for example. Javed is from Afghanistan, a country soaked for many generations in a culture of revenge. Revenge is a way of life. But once Javed became Christ's follower, his worldview was challenged by God's transforming Word which told him to love his enemies. So the next time someone insults him, what will he do? Will he forgive as the Bible says, or take revenge as his old lens says? As these two worldviews have a wrestling match in his head, which will he obey? If he chooses to go God's way and forgive, he will become one step more like Jesus. If he takes revenge, he will go one step back.

---

[11] Romans 12:1, NLT.

Our view of God

Underlying so much of how we see the world is how we see God. It is for this reason that experienced disciplers drill right down to the nature of God as a core concept in building a new worldview. Recall from Chapter 4 how Pastor Ian in Leicester suddenly found Afghans and Iranians turning up at church. His discipling approach is this: "We basically teach them get their roots down into God, into the love of the Father, into Jesus, into relationship with Holy Spirit. Get your roots down into him and you will be strong."[12]

Knowing God as Father is a particularly big step for many of Muslim background. Bilquis Sheikh, in her famous book *I Dared to Call Him Father*, describes the moment when, still a Muslim, she followed a Christian's advice to speak to God in this way:

Bilquis Sheikh (in Pakistan)

"Oh Father, my Father". Hesitantly, I spoke His name aloud (...) "Father, oh my Father God", I cried, with growing confidence (....) He was there! I could sense His Presence. I could feel His hand laid gently on my head. It was as if I could see His eyes, filled with love and compassion. He was so close that I found myself laying my head on His knees like a little girl sitting at her father's feet. For a long time I knelt there, sobbing quietly, floating in His love. [13]

Even after coming to faith in Christ, it may still take a long time for a former Muslim securely to know God as heavenly Father. This was especially difficult for Hannah Shah, author of *The Imam's Daughter*,[14] since in childhood she had suffered serious abuse by her father:

Hannah Shah

The fatherhood of God has been a lifelong journey for me. As a new believer I couldn't sing the words "Father God I wonder how I managed to exist without the knowledge of your parenthood and your loving care". It was partly because of the abuse but also the image of God in Islam. Over time, the Christian men in my life have helped me redefine what 'father' means, especially my adopted dad who gave me a tiny glimpse of how God sees me. But I wouldn't say I have ever been comfortable with that. A worship song in church recently, "You are a good, good Father" left me spent and in tears, along with the sense of his presence and him wanting desperately for me to feel that.[15]

---

12 *Joining the Family* course.
13 Bilquis Sheikh, *I Dared to Call Him Father*, (Kingsway, 1978).
14 Hannah Shah, *The Imam's Daughter*, (Rider 2009).
15 Personal communication.

What part can we play in this transforming process?

Transformation doesn't happen automatically, for it's perfectly possible to memorise Bible verses in one mental compartment while isolating this from the actual worldview we live by. Real change starts when God's Word is brought into crunching contact with the old mental attitude, so that the contrast is unavoidable. We can help our BMB friend in this, by bringing relevant Bible passages to bear on particular issues they face; not in a scolding way, but by exploring the implications together.

Often opportunities come up informally to bring God's 'lens' to bear on these life-issues. Jan finds this with her friend of Muslim background: "We might be shopping, and something may come up that will give a way in to a biblical concept, and we can mention it then and say, 'When we get home we can look at it later' ".[16]

Alongside this, structured Bible courses are also needed. One advantage of a structured discipleship course is that it helps to ensure you and your friend actually get down to study God's Word together in a regular way. Especially useful are courses that don't just teach doctrine (important though that is) but also bring it to bear on worldview issues. That's why, when I wrote the discipleship course *Come Follow Me*, I sought to bring the teaching of 1 Peter to grapple with some common attitudes of Muslims in a particular conservative culture. I used actual examples and even pictures to make the teaching more concrete, as a springboard for discussion between the new believer and the person mentoring them. Alternatively, a whole group can go through the course together, so that BMBs are learning from each other and not just from a mentor. This group interaction takes the learning through to another level and reduces dependence on the 'discipler'.

So let's try to balance the spontaneous use of God's Word with some systematic Bible study as well. All of scripture is useful for "teaching, rebuking, correcting and training in righteousness"[17] – as well as for encouraging, assuring and comforting. So we can use any part of the Bible:

- *The Gospels* are full of vivid illustrations, and stories, and examples of how Jesus related to both men and women;
- *Acts* is a foundational book for showing how to follow Christ by his Spirit in his community;
- *The Epistles* were written as discipleship manuals for new believers and contain wonderful promises to memorise as anchors for the soul;
- *Old Testament* passages give key examples of heroes of faith, building on the brief references to them in the Qur'an;
- *The Psalms* give a believer words (and permission) to express honestly to God how worried or joyful or angry or frustrated or grateful they are feeling.

---

16 *Joining the Family* course.
17 2 Timothy 3:16. NIV.

So we need a mix from the whole of God's Word. Bear in mind that concrete examples and life-stories arise in narrative sections but also can be used to illustrate other parts of scripture; they help a believer grasp hold of abstract concepts. BMBs assume that scripture is to be obeyed literally, so don't be surprised by a question like "Why do Christians eat pork when this is forbidden in Leviticus?" For the same reason, they may struggle with the Old Testament's emphasis on Israel and Zion and this needs unpacking sensitively. Unfamiliar terms like 'baptism' also need explaining – and familiar religious terminology may need explaining even more! This is because whenever you use a label like 'God' or 'sin' or 'prophet', familiar words for those of Muslim background, their brain will naturally connect those labels with their Islamic meanings. So new biblical meanings are needed: new concepts for old labels.

In Chapter 5 the mobile phone was described as an important way to keep in touch with our friend on a frequent basis. It is also becoming an ever-more-important tool in discipleship. Today most BMBs in the West can access the internet through their phone, and the world of useful apps is expanding rapidly. Here are some ways to use mobiles and digital media in discipleship, with a few specific examples in Appendix 1:

- Send your friend a daily Bible verse or word of encouragement;
- Show them how to read the Bible on their phone in their mother tongue;
- Meet with them on skype whenever it's not possible face to face;
- Point them to websites with Christian songs, teaching and forums in their own language;
- Find websites with discipleship courses designed specifically for believers of Muslim background.

4) An active Christian role

There's a real danger of seeing Christians of Muslim heritage just as passive recipients of teaching, pastoral care and practical support. To be sure, all new believers need plenty of support at the beginning, and those of Muslim background are no exception. But it's not healthy to stay permanently in that place. It's not good for the mentoring relationship, which stays lopsided and paternalistic: "We give, they receive". It's not good for the church, which gets deprived of what that believer can bring. And it's not good for the person himself or herself, since having an active role is an important part of belonging and growing.

My Iranian friend Fafar found that having an active role helped her from early on in her Christian life. She helped in arranging the flowers for church and serving coffee after the service; this gave her a sense of being useful, and belonging. From there she went on to other responsibilities like helping to lead an Alpha course. Two other BMB ladies had a similar experience:

Shieva (from Iran)

Serving at the local church helped me a lot to grow. I started leading the worship and also doing other practical stuff in between. The thing that was really amazing for me was that my pastor trusted me and he gave me responsibility. One day he said to me, "I feel I should give the responsibility of leading the worship to you". I was so overwhelmed, and I accepted it. And while leading the worship I was just learning and experiencing new things. That helped me a lot.[18]

Favour (from Nigeria)
The local church has really, really equipped me. When they see a gift, they just pick it up and help you. I teach a baptismal class, and there is this particular occasion that really struck me. I wasn't feeling too well that day and physically I was struggling for strength. After the lesson I thought it was rubbish. But at the next class, this beautiful girl just started crying. I asked "What happened, are you okay?" She said, "The lesson from last week made my life". And I just said to God, "Thank you, thank you, this can only be you".[19]

Active Christian roles are not just restricted to church activities. I think of three such believers in my home town who have grown tremendously through doing boid evangelism on the streets, with a book-table. As we will see in Chapter 9, in some situations believers need to be careful in public witness because of their Muslim relatives, and no one should push them into it. But equally, no one should hold them back from it if the time is right and they themselves feel the inner urge.

5) Experiencing God personally
We long for our friends of Muslim background to grow strong in him. We wrestle in prayer for them to "firm in all the will of God, mature and fully assured", as Epaphras did for the believers at Colossae.[20] But whatever efforts we make to help them grow in Christ, in the end they must take responsibility for their own walk with God – just as I must be responsible for mine. Favour puts it this way:

Favour (from Nigeria)
It's important for the church to help me grow as a believer, but it's very important to me as a person individually to develop that relationship with Jesus. The church is very, very important in showing me the way, but it's also left for me, at night when the church is not there, to say, "I love Jesus. I want to know him, I want to have fellowship with him".[21]

---

18 *Joining the Family* course.
19 *Joining the Family* course.
20 Colossians 4:12, NIV.
21 *Joining the Family* course.

When times are tough, our dear BMB friends need to prove in their own direct experience that the Bible's God is their God too. They need to depend first-hand on his promises, not just second-hand via their Christian friend's faith. They need a personal faith which, like gold, is tested and purified by fire. They need to experience the thrill of answered prayer. They need to walk by the Spirit, to trust and obey, to fail and fall and come back to God again and push on stronger than before.

Aren't those the very same ways in which we grew in our own experience of God? It's no different for those of Muslim background. Roxy initially received a lot of hands-on support and care as a teenage new believer. Later, when she went away to university, she had to rely on God for herself:

Roxy

In my personal experience of God, my walk with God, a significant moment was when I first moved away from the significant people and relationships I had first started my Christian journey with, and I was on my own. Suddenly we have this time when we have to dig in ourselves to God. It is good for us, it helps us grow us in confidence, and it thrusts us out of our comfort zone. This helped me know that wherever I am, in whatever circumstances, I am able to read the Bible for myself, I'm able to pray, I'm able to become part of a different church and build those relationships of community without the help of those who were with me at the beginning. It makes it more personal, being tested in that way.[22]

Discipleship is "a long obedience in the same direction".[23] It will be proved in our daily walk with God as well as in unexpected times of crisis. It cannot be short-cut and no one else can do it for us, nor for our friend of Muslim background. We can and should walk alongside them but we cannot walk on behalf of them.

6) Other growth factors

In this chapter we have considered five of the most important factors by which BMBs typically grow in Christ:

- An individual mentor
- The community of believers
- God's transforming Word
- An active Christian role
- Experiencing God personally

We could have mentioned other factors too. There is *baptism*, which can strengthen a believer's confidence of being bonded to Christ and to his people.

---

22 Personal conversation, as we worked on this book together.
23 This phrase was coined by Eugene Petersen in his book of the same name (IVP 2010).

A certain measure of *opposition* can stiffen resolve, though persecution is not to be sought out and too much of it can be psychologically damaging. *A Christian spouse* can play a key role as a rock of affirmation when rejected by one's own Muslim relatives, and as a doorway into a new Christian family. For those reared in Islam but coming to Christ, *life structure* is a particularly important factor, as we will see in Chapter 8. To read further on these and other growth factors, see the related section in 'Recommended Resources', Appendix 1.

The all-important growth factor

God has not designed us to the same identikit pattern and he works differently in all of our lives. But there is one all-important factor we see in all cases of genuine Christian growth, the factor St. Paul describes here:

> *The Lord - who is the Spirit - makes us more and more like him as we are changed into his glorious image.*[24]

To help our friend grow up into fullness in Christ, we as humans can play our part, and it's an important part. But the one indispensable factor is God himself, who works within our friend's life by his Spirit. However passionately we care for our friends of Muslim background, they are not our own disciples. They are Jesus' disciples. We point them to Jesus but ultimately we can't take his place in their lives. They need to depend on him not on us. Therefore we need "an unswerving faith in the power of God to bring them through"[25].

Gordon Hickson (a friend and mentor of BMBs)

You can't control somebody, they've got to be able to be released and you've got to trust them and encourage them. Sometimes people hold on too tightly when they are discipling a person. There's got to be a sense that you trust them to go to hell and back. Sometimes they've got to make a mess and then you've got to pick them up, get them back on the road and encourage them. And if you keep on doing that, the parenting finally releases them and they go further than you have ever been.[26]

"Further than you have ever been". Now that's an exciting vision, isn't it?

---

24 2 Corinthians 3:18, NLT.
25 Jan in *Joining the Family* course.
26 *Joining the Family* course.

POINTS TO PONDER:

1 What things helped you grow in Christ? Compare those growth factors with the ones described in this chapter for Christ's followers of Muslim background. What similarities and differences do you see?

2 "Imitate me as I imitate Christ". How do you feel about being a role model for other believers including those of Muslim background? Pray about this.

3 If you have a BMB friend, ask them how they would like you to help them grow in Christ.

Joining the Family

CHAPTER EIGHT

Life structure

(Tim writing...)

This book has discussed the loss of identity and loss of community which Muslim people so often experience in coming to Christ, and how they seek to rebuild those things in Christ. There is a third big loss, often felt keenly by BMBs but not so obvious to onlookers: the loss of an ordered life structure.

Why does 'life structure' matter so much to Christ's followers of Muslim heritage? Let's start by listening to two of them. Karim from East Africa and Ziya from Turkey had very different upbringings, yet they each faced the same dilemma after turning to Christ.

Karim

In Islam, we have set times of prayers, everything is regulated: how you sleep, what you eat, when you eat, who you give to, how much you give, who you marry, everything. And you come to Christianity, and it looks so chaotic. You think over and over, "Where are the guidelines, what am I going to do, when do I read the Bible, when do I pray? And what do I do with this situation?" It's a very, very difficult position for a new believer to be in.[1]

Ziya

Most of the guidelines in life, from what to wear, to what to eat are replaced with a confusing 'freedom in Christ'. The new convert, devoid of any religious rituals and regulations, often feels lost.[2]

---

1   *Joining the Family* course
2   Ziya Meral, 'Conversion and Apostasy: A Sociological Perspective', (*Evangelical Missions Quarterly*, *Vol* 42, 2006), p. 511.

Finding a new life structure in Christ is a more important aspect of discipleship than Western Christians usually realise, especially Protestant Christians. This chapter helps us to understand this better, and to think about patterns and spiritual disciplines which might be helpful to your friend but without merely substituting a new set of 'rules' in place of the old.

Islam's secure life structure

Islam places a big emphasis on what it calls *shariah*. This is typically translated as 'law', but is much more than just law in the Western sense of the word. Rather, it is an all-embracing framework which aims to cover every aspect of a Muslim's life, from morning to night and from the cradle to the grave. It is "the detailed code of conduct for Muslims to follow, both in their private and public lives", writes a Muslim scholar Kateregga. He continues:

Kateregga
The Shari'ah instructs man on how he should eat, receive visitors, buy and sell, slaughter animals, clean himself, sleep, go to the toilet, lead a government, practise justice, pray and perform other acts of ibadat (worship).[3]

On this definition, the scope of *shariah* includes everything from 'going to the toilet' to 'leading a government'. There is to be no distinction between the sacred and the secular; all of life is to be lived under God's sovereign rule.

This level of detail may seem restrictive to a Westerner, but for many Muslims it offers the comfort of clear guidelines. It tells them what is 'allowed' and what is 'forbidden'. In fact, in a permissive society which knows no boundaries, some Westerners too are attracted to Islam's secure life structure. One British Muslim convert said, "With Islam, there is not this burden of weighing things up. There are obligations and you do them. It is very liberating".[4] These converts are glad to have swapped choice for structure.

'A confusing freedom in Christ'

Meanwhile, those who convert from Islam to Christ have gone in the opposite direction. They have swapped Islam's secure life structure for a faith which has far fewer specific rules. So what are they supposed to do with what Ziya called "a confusing freedom in Christ"? Other BMBs also found this a struggle at first:

---

3 Kateregga & Shenk: *Islam and Christianity*, Uzima Press, Kenya (1980), pg.67.
4 Umm Rashid in P. Stanford, 'Preaching from the Converted'. *Independent on Sunday*, 16 May 2004, cited in Katherine Zebiri, *British Muslim Converts: Choosing Alternative Lives*, (Oneworld 2007), p.91.

Chris (who grew up in Pakistan)

When I became a new believer, everything was new for me. I had to learn a completely new lifestyle. Everything that I had learned from childhood I had to abandon. I had to learn a new way of praying, I had to make new friends, and so everything was new. So that was the biggest challenge.[5]

Khalida (British BMB)

When I became a Christian I found it really difficult not conforming to my old way of worshipping God, which was about fasting religiously and also praying five times a day. I found that a struggle, to have all that freedom in worship. Being able to pray at any moment of the day, having this amazing relationship with God, where you could hear him, you could feel and sense his love for you and experience his presence, it's quite overwhelming but in a really lovely way. But having that freedom, I think that would be a bit of a struggle for believers from a Muslim background.

Samy (BMB pastor)

At first, Christianity can be seen as a very liberal religion and one where we have the liberty to make choices, and yet still be accepted. That was conceivably the most off-putting thing that I found about Christianity. As a Muslim I saw Christianity as a Mickey Mouse religion…

Later Samy realised that Christianity, far from being a "Mickey Mouse religion", is actually "a way of life that is incredibly demanding". But some new Christians coming from Islam are dazzled by the apparent freedom. Then they may go off in either of two unhelpful directions. In their search for a new framework they may simply create a new set of rules as legalistic as the old ones. Alternatively, and more commonly, they may throw off rules altogether; they enjoy their new-found freedom but fail to develop habits and structures which would help them grow strong in Christ.

Questions of culture

If culture is a society's whole way of life…
… and if *shariah* spells out an ordered way of life for a whole society…
… then inevitably *shariah* is as much about culture as it is about law.

---

5 *Joining the Family* course

In principle, Islam seeks to standardise many aspects of culture. This includes codes of diet and dress, for example. I have lived and travelled widely in the Muslim world, and arriving in any new Muslim country I feel at home because the cultural symbols are so familiar. Women cover their heads and alcohol is not openly for sale, for example. Muslim cultures that deviate from this are seen by the purists as 'unIslamic', since *shariah* lays down the standard. *Shariah* also elevates the place of Arabic language, so the religious vocabulary in most Muslim countries is derived from Arabic. Also, Arab culture is assumed to be more authentically 'Islamic', which is why Arab styles of women's head covering have spread worldwide along with the Islamic revival, even though other styles would be equally acceptable in theory.

Does this mean that all Muslim culture is tinged by *shariah* and must be rejected by the new Christian? Actually, it's not that simple. For one thing, the values affirmed in Muslim cultures are also strong in other collectivist societies: such as hospitality, shared decision making and respect for elders. These values should not be rejected when a Muslim turns to Christ, for they are upheld in Scripture too, and they shine a searching light on our Western cultures. Secondly, the gospel affirms cultural variety. The early church leaders made the decision – a monumentally important decision for the future of Christianity - to allow non-Jewish believers to follow Jesus with the minimum of cultural change. They declared that a few Gentile practices would have to be *rejected* but most could be *retained*.[6] This principle applies to other non-Christian cultures including Muslim cultures, while bearing in mind that retained practices may also need to be *reinterpreted*. It's not just about banning or allowing a particular cultural activity, but about how that activity is interpreted in different people's minds. For example, what did eating meat which had been sacrificed to idols mean to the individual Christians in Corinth, what did it mean to their fellow-believers and how did it appear to their non-Christian neighbours? Should believers reject, retain or renew the practice?

Similar questions arise in any country where the gospel begins to make headway in a non-Christian culture. Which elements of their inherited culture should Christ's followers reject, which should they retain and which should they reinterpret? Europe was Christianised so long ago that we forget that the gospel pioneers and the first believers asked just the same questions. Indeed these issues always will arise for first generation believers of any non-Christian background. In the past missionaries encountered them in far-off lands, but now we all live in a pluralist society and so we must think this through for ourselves. When people of Muslim, Hindu and Sikh cultures start turning to Christ, or for that matter 'yuppies' or 'Goths', they bring their cultures with them. This can set up tensions in church life just as it did in the early church when Gentiles

---

6   This is just a bare bald way to summarise the Acts 15 decision, but I realise the missiological issues are more complex than this and they continue to be hotly debated. There is not space here to expand on that debate.

started joining a previously Jewish church. But the early Christians found a way through and were enriched by it. So must we.

Take, for example, the question of diet. We love our ham and bacon, but Muslims see them as repulsive. In other cultures large, crunchy cockroaches are a delicacy, but I would find them repulsive. Actually as a Christian I *am allowed* to eat cockroaches, but this doesn't mean I *want* to. In the same way Muslims who become Christ's followers are now free to eat pork, but it doesn't mean they will want to. It's their choice. Don't view them as less 'Christian' if they prefer not to. Nor should we judge them on what they wear. An English pastor asked a Pakistani new believer when she would stop wearing what he called 'Muslim clothes'. All she was wearing was her normal Pakistani outfit which everyone wears in Pakistan including the Christians!

I wrote the discipleship course *Come Follow Me* as a relational tool for mentors helping BMBs to grow strong in their faith. In the advisors guide are 'cultural clues' which may be helpful for mentors who know little of Muslim cultures. But they are only generalisations, and Muslim cultures vary, so the most useful thing will be to ask your friend about their own particular viewpoint. Don't assume beforehand which cultural practices a believer of Muslim background should retain, reject or reinterpret. Instead, first discuss with your friend what that practice means to them personally, and how it appears to others, and only then consider what biblical principles may be relevant. Thus if your BMB friend still wears a headscarf in church, you might ask what this means to her, then discuss how it appears to others and what biblical principles apply. If you wear a miniskirt, she and you can go through the same process. In this way, as believers of different cultures hold up mirrors to each other, it exposes our blindspots and helps us understand each other more generously.

The book *Notes for the Journey* is subtitled *Following Jesus, staying South Asian*. 'South Asia' means the Indian sub-continent from where many Muslims, Hindus, Sikhs and others have come to Britain. When people of those religious backgrounds turn to Christ, how can they work out which aspects of their culture to reject, which to retain and which to reinterpret? This book has many wise insights, particularly by showing how similar issues arise across these different religious backgrounds in a Western setting. "We need to pray and act according to our conscience, in a way that honours God and shows love to our family and friends", it advises.[7]

The law of love

It's hard-wired into Protestant Christianity to affirm that, "We are not under law but under grace". True enough, so long as it's not cheap grace. This is the grace of Christ who bought us back at great price and to whom we belong totally.

---

7   C. Rasiah and Robin Thomson, editors, *Notes for the Journey: Following Jesus, staying South Asian*, (South Asian Concern, 2011), p.53

Therefore as believers we are under law in a different way, i.e. we are under a solemn obligation to live for our Master and not for ourselves.

This notion is very important to make clear to our BMB friends who previously as Muslims saw obedience to *shariah* as a way to earn religious merit, but who now find themselves 'free in Christ'. To clarify the difference between Islamic and biblical concepts of serving our Master, I use this imaginary story in the *Come Follow Me* course[8]. This story comes in the lesson 'The Law of Love' and is set in a traditional Muslim country.

Two young men met in the market. Both were servants, and their masters had sent them to do the shopping. They started talking about their masters. "I try hard to please my master", said the first servant, "but I never know when he will get angry. I am afraid of his punishment".

"I too try to please my master", replied the other servant. "But I do it out of love, not out of fear. You see, my father was killed in the war and my mother died of cancer. I had to beg in the streets. One day a kind man found me and brought me to his home. He has done so much for me and even lets me eat at his table. I love him because he first loved me".

"I wish I could love my master", commented the first servant.[9]

This is just an imaginary story, but it helps us see how we are indeed bound to obey our Master, not from fear but from gratitude for all he has done for us. "You are not your own, you were bought at a price. Therefore honour God with your bodies"[10] is the memory verse for that session in *Come Follow Me*.

Once a legal expert asked Jesus which was the most important commandment in the Law of Moses. "You shall love the Lord your God with all your heart and with all your soul and with all your mind and with all your strength", replied Jesus, "and you shall love your neighbor as yourself".[11] This summary of Christ's *shariah* (if we may use the term) is easy to recite but extremely hard to obey! We can only

---

8   More information on the course is in http://www.bmbtraining.org/cfm-2/cfm-course-manual/
9   Some modern Muslims in the West emphasise Allah's love. We must listen to their viewpoint, yet I find nothing in Islam to parallel Christ's self-giving on the cross or the full certainty of sins forgiven. Recently in Oxford I was chatting with a Muslim shop assistant selling me some shoes. "I pray five times a day and fast in Ramadan", he told me, "yet still I go to bed every night scared of God's judgement". And modern Muslim websites debate how we can 'earn' Allah's love.
10 1 Corinthians 6:19-20, NIV.
11 Mark 12:30-31, NIV.

love because God first loved us, and only in the power of his Spirit. The sincere Muslim has the laudable *aim* to obey God fully in every area of life. But the gospel gives us the *challenge* that love is the highest form of obedience, along with the *motivation* to do this and the *power* to do so.

Islam's *shariah* works from the outside inwards, changing our behaviour first in the hope it will also change our heart. Christ's *shariah* starts on the inside by changing our heart, but this must then work its way outwards to our behaviour too. Javed explains this point in his own words:

Javed (Afghan Christian worker)

When you read the story of Jesus it's even harder than the law of Moses, but the good thing about being in Christ, is that we don't have to strive to do all those things. By the guidance and by the power of the Holy Spirit, we live from the inside out, not from the outside in. So when I was a Muslim, I was trying to get to God and trying to please him, but now when I was filled with the Holy Spirit, I do it anyway because that's part of my nature. I don't have to strive, because I'm living under the guidance of the Holy Spirit.[12]

In the animal world, some creatures like beetles have an 'exo-skeleton', where the firm structure is on the outside. By contrast mammals and birds have an 'endo-skeleton' with bones on the inside of their bodies. The big danger comes if a Muslim loses a kind of exo-skeleton on becoming Christ's follower, but fails to grow a new and different endo-skeleton in its place. That leaves them in a vulnerable place with no 'skeleton' at all.

Islam's five pillars

The five 'pillars' of Islam are foundational and deeply embedded in the consciousness of Muslim people. They provide an ordered framework for individuals and society:

Five pillars of Islam   summarised here by Tom and Judi Walsh

1. The creed *(shahada)*, whispered into the ears of a new born Muslim and the final words a dying person would hope to hear, is constantly on the lips of devout Muslims. It is used in the call to prayer and welcomes new converts into the Muslim community.

2. The prayer liturgy *(salat)* is recited by observant Muslims five times a day. This communal activity is heavily structured with set times, Mecca as the direction of prayer and compulsory ablutions. Those who pray

---

12   *Joining the Family* course.

incorrectly are put right, as it is important that the ritual is followed appropriately according to Islamic tradition.

3. Likewise there is a clear and precise expectation of giving **the charity-tax** *(zakat)* which each Muslim is expected to follow, offering 2.5% of their disposable wealth each year.

4. **The month of fasting** known as Ramadan is an especially important month in the Islamic calendar. From dawn to dusk Muslims refuse all food and drink. This allows for thanksgiving and reflection; they seek reconciliation with God and others; they yearn for closeness to God and holiness; it reminds them of the needy and it expresses great solidarity with other Muslims.

5. The final pillar of Islam is the obligatory once in a lifetime **pilgrimage to Mecca** known as *Hajj.* Very precise directions are given to each traveller over the three day period, visiting key Islamic sites around Mecca and remembering key moments in the life of Mohammed. It is for many the pinnacle of their Muslim experience.

So for many Muslims there is a daily, monthly, annual even lifelong ritual to be followed and obeyed. The teaching and practice is clear and simple. They know what to do.

Alternative 'pillars'?

Given the loss of order and framework which comes from abandoning these pillars, is it helpful to suggest to BMBs some Christian equivalents? Or is it merely confusing? I experimented with this in the *Come Follow Me* course. I found that this approach does work, so long as we stress the fundamental difference between an 'exo-skeleton' with specific external rules to follow and an 'endo-skeleton' which provides hidden structure from the inside. For example, in the lesson on prayer I emphasised the difference between the Islamic prayer-ritual at set times of day and in set words, and the freedom Christ's followers have to come to their heavenly Father at any time. Likewise, instead of fasting at fixed times of day in a fixed month, Christians are free to fast in any way at any time.

Of course the danger of teaching liberty is that it so easily leads to laxity. If believers are taught "you no longer have to give the charity-tax and it's up to you how much you give", they may never learn the joy of sacrificial giving. So how may we remain flexible in our Christian practices as the New Testament affirms, while still having the self-discipline to grow a strong inner 'skeleton'? Judi Walsh, in discipling women believers of Muslim background, comments:

Judi

There is a sense in which spiritual disciplines are so healthy for us and build our relationship with God, but I unpack with these women the motivation that lies behind doing them, breaking away from doing it from duty but doing it out of love and choice, and spending the time with God.[13]

Judi and her husband Tom serve with The Navigators, a Christian organisation which has helped millions of Christians to develop a healthy yet joyous life structure as disciples of Jesus. As experienced mentors of BMBs, Tom and Judi discuss spiritual disciplines and then other aspects of life structure, for the rest of this chapter.

(Tom and Judi writing…)

Building a healthy life structure

Life structure touches on all of aspects of a person: spiritual, mental, emotional and physical. When a Muslim becomes a follower of Jesus, they have experienced a profound turning and have recognised the good news of Jesus Christ. This good news is not the law as they know it but a free gift – grace – salvation is theirs, undeserved, unearned, unmerited. What joy many experience! What freedom in Christ!

But now what do they *do*? All their lives, whether devout or not, they have lived with an assured structure that Islam has given to them. So now they want to know if there is something which Christianity or Christ demands of them? For many this is a time of difficult transition and questions, and so people in church need to be able to help them in this new journey.

The answer to their question "Do we have to *do* anything to be Christian?" is ironically both a 'no' and a 'yes'. 'No' in the sense that the gospel of grace is indeed a free gift which no one can work for. In Christ every believer is a new creation seen by God as his loved child, part of the flock. God cannot love us anymore than he already does. He sees us in Christ as spotless and clean; our honour, lost because of sin, is now restored. One of the scandals of the gospel message is that all this comes totally free.

So in what sense is 'yes' also an answer to the question "Do we have to *do* anything?" This answer is tied up with the notion of discipleship. A disciple is simply a follower or a learner; an apprentice of a master. Likewise a Christian is simply a disciple of their master Jesus Christ. Indeed the word 'Christian' is hardly ever used in the Bible. Initially it was just a term of abuse ascribed to

---

13 *Joining the Family* course.

early Christians by their enemies, and is mentioned just three times in the New Testament. By contrast the word 'disciple' is used 269 times! "The New Testament is a book about disciples, by disciples, and for disciples of Jesus Christ", writes Dallas Willard.[14] He explains that when this biblical norm was later replaced by the idea of conversion and membership, it weakened the thought of religious instruction, for if a convert belonged to the community that was considered enough. Even today some regard conversion as the ultimate success in their story with Muslim friends.

This is never the goal, however, according to the Bible. Paul maintains that maturity in Christ is the real aim:

> *He is the one we proclaim, admonishing and teaching everyone with all wisdom, so that we may present everyone fully mature in Christ. To this end I strenuously contend with all the energy Christ so powerfully works in me.* [15]

In his final letter to Timothy, Paul describes the Christian as being like a soldier on duty, not being distracted away from the priority of pleasing his commanding officer, but rather enduring the hardship one might face in this line of work. In the same passage he refers to athletes who are seeking to win the garland of victory and farmers labouring hard to produce a good crop. All of these occupations demonstrate commitment and discipline in order to achieve the goals set.

Spiritual disciplines

So the thoughts behind the word 'disciple' convey a dynamic learner, one who wants to progress in the faith, one who wants to copy the way of his Master and one who is committed. Certain disciplines can help this disciple to learn, grow and flourish. There is value in daily routines and disciplines as long as we don't allow them to become padlocks which imprison us again. Routines and disciplines are just a framework, not an end in themselves or something to be imposed.

In the rest of this section, we attempt to propose or suggest some spiritual disciplines which we have found very helpful. We must stress the fact that these disciplines do not make the person more loved by Christ; they are not a way of trying to make God love us more than he does already. They are instead a statement of our commitment to want to be a disciple of Jesus Christ, and the intention that whatever happens we will pursue Him.

---

14   Dallas Willard, *The Spirit of the Disciplines.*
15   Colossians 1:28-29, NIV.

The Wheel illustration[16]

This illustration has given us the basis o
over forty years of following Christ and
helps us reflect as to how we are doing.
It provides a nice rounded structure for
suggesting spiritual disciplines helpful
to the new believer. Each part of this
illustration represents a crucially important
component of a vibrant Christian life -
from the Christ-centred hub, to the rim
representing obedience to Christ, to each of
the four spokes of witnessing, prayer, fellowship
and the Word. Let's explore each how part of the
wheel might help believers from a Muslim background to enter deeply into a
discipleship relationship with Christ.

'The Hub': Christ the centre

Total surrender to Christ's authority and lordship is not always a decision made
right at conversion, but is a necessary act of will. For the believer, the "old life"
has gone and the new has come, and Christ dwells through us instead.[17] God
creates within us the desire to do what he wants us to do in order to express his
lordship in our lives. One of the best ways to express this commitment to Christ
is the daily act of having a space for him, to give him a portion of time to reflect
and think and be quiet before him. This discipline, sometimes called the Quiet
Time, often can begin the Christian's day.

A 'quiet time' is simply being intentional about having a conversation with
God - listening for God's voice by reading the Bible or devotions, and speaking
to God through prayer. Jesus did this numerous times in the Gospels, sometimes
slipping away all night or in the early morning, to spend time with his Father.
There are no real rules for having a Quiet Time - what matters is to be spending
time with Christ. We often ask ourselves two questions after a reading: "Who are
you, Lord?" and "What do you want me to do, Lord?" This keeps the Quiet Time
personal and practical as well as prayerful. God is pleased when we give him the
first portions of our day, and the regular act of having a Quiet Time will help the
new believer stay centered on Christ at the beginning of each day.

Two vertical 'Spokes': How we relate to God

The Word

The Word of God, the Bible, is his direct voice showing us not only who he is,
but how to live and interact with everyone around us, so an earnest personal

---

16 It was developed first by a Christian organisation called The Navigators.

17 2 Corinthians 5:17, Galatians 2:20.

intake of God's Word is essential for health and growth.[18] Through the Scriptures, we can see God's principles for life and ministry, learn how to obey him and become acquainted with the Christ who is worth of our steadfast allegiance. How do we take in scripture in a way that is meaningful and manageable? We can *hear* it from godly teachers, *read* it systematically, *study* it on our own or with others, *memorise* it and *meditate* on it. By committing oneself to these various methods of receiving God's word a good firm hold is developed in our use and understanding of the scriptures.

Prayer

Prayer is our natural response to God as we hear him speak through his Word. It is sharing our heart with the One who longs for our companionship and who cares about our concerns. Prayer not only trains our hearts and minds to know God's power and glory, but also turns his ear towards action in our lives and of those who we pray for.[19] As Paul says, "Pray in the Spirit on all occasions with all kinds of prayers and requests. With this in mind, be alert and always keep on praying for all the Lord's people." [20]

Many believers find that prayer, especially spending long amounts of time in prayer, can be one of the hardest parts of spiritual discipline. For some the very simple acronym ACTS is a good way to remember these different ways of praying – Adoration, Confession, Thanksgiving and Supplication. A balanced prayer life developed over time by the new believer will include a variety of ways of praying at one time or another.

Two horizontal 'Spokes': How we relate to others

Fellowship

In the Wheel diagram, the spokes of 'fellowship' and 'witnessing' refer to our horizontal relationships with other people. God has directed Christians to build each other up in fellowship through inter-dependent, loving relationships with each other. Gathering together as the Body of Christ draws God close around us as we praise him and encourage one another.[21] The prayer of Jesus in John 17 shows how much he longs for his disciples to be united, loving and one. There are no lone rangers in the Christian life. Being in a church, Christian community or fellowship is absolutely essential to growth. God can and does miraculously provide for Christians who through no fault of their own are isolated and cut off from fellowship. But this is not the norm. Fellowship is possibly the most important spoke of all in the Wheel Illustration for it combines all the other spokes in one way or another.

---

18 2 Timothy 3:16, Joshua 1:8
19 John 15:7, Philippians 4:6-7
20 Ephesians 6:19, NIV.
21 Hebrews 10:24-25, Matthew 18:20.

Witnessing

God has given believers the joy and responsibility of telling the world about the Good News of Christ's work on earth. Sharing this spectacular news with others should be the natural overflow of a rich, vibrant life in Christ.[22] However, for those of Muslim background, where apostasy can be seen as bringing shame and dishonour to the family and community, an open witness to Christ can be a very real problem. Indeed, for a number of new believers there may well be real danger in the act of publicly identifying themselves as Christians. Therefore great care and sensitivity needs to be used. Equally damaging may be using the novelty of having a believer from a Muslim background in a congregation. As young Christians they may be put up on pedestals before they are ready, asked repeatedly to tell their story of conversion, with the danger that pride may overtake and ultimately destroy their Christian life.

So whilst in the heart of every new believer there is a natural desire to speak to others about Christ we would urge caution here in the first instance. Jesus told Nicodemus, a man who came to Jesus secretly at night[23] that becoming a Christian was like being born again. When we think of new babies we do indeed think of beautiful new creations. However these new and lovely people can sometimes make a real mess, in a way that adults have learned not to do. They are particularly vulnerable at this point in their lives and need nurturing and care before they can develop into the healthy beings God intends them to be. Many people including myself have regretted too hastily returning to their families and spilling out the gospel message to a critical, unresponsive audience. Perhaps a better way of progressing is to live the life first, showing the transformation that the gospel message has brought, and loving friends and family in ways that surprise, baffle and make them want to ask questions.[24] If they love people they previously didn't care for, and are willing to forgive when hurt or insulted, and do good things they previously weren't known for, and speak well and wisely, free from cursing and swearing, these are all massively life changing phenomena that other people will notice. With time the new believer will become more familiar with the gospel message itself and how to explain it in a way that makes sense to their Muslim family and friends.

It may be very useful for the new believer to have their testimony written out and memorised. Paul's testimony in Acts 22 provides a helpful threefold template to follow, of "before I accepted Christ", "how I received Christ" and "after I accepted Christ". Having a prepared testimony is a good way for a new believer to be ready to share their story with friends and family. Believers of Muslim background might be wise to practice on safe people initially, those they know personally and who understand their need for delicacy in this matter.

---

22 Matthew 4:19, Romans 1:16.
23 John 3.
24 Peter's advice is helpful: "Revere Christ as Lord. Always be prepared to give an answer to everyone who asks you to give the reason for the hope that you have. But do this with gentleness and respect." 1 Peter 3:15, NIV.

'The Rim': Obedience to Christ

Some acts of obedience to God are internal, such as attitudes, habits, motives, values and day-to-day thoughts. But even these eventually surface outwardly in our relationships with other people. Obeying Christ's commandments is our outward indication of inward health and love for Christ - our worship.[25] Loving God and other people is the true mark of a Christian. What a challenge! James urged his hearers, "Do not merely listen to the word, and so deceive yourselves. Do what it says." [26]

The wonderful thing, as we reflect on the work of a wheel, is that when it is doing its job properly it is helping to move something. It is not static or still. The spokes are hardly noticed when a wheel is turning – what gets noticed is the rim and the hub. That's how it should be in the Christian life. Christ becomes the focal point in the life of the new disciple and it is Christ that other people notice. They do not necessarily see the disciplines of time spent alone with God in prayer and study of the Bible, in fellowship with other Christians. Instead, with the help of the disciplines, people will end up seeing a transformed life lived out of a transforming message.

Summary

As well as these spiritual disciplines encompassed in the Wheel illustration, it is also good for Christians to engage in other disciplines such as resting and working, fasting, giving, journaling, silence and solitude.[27] A believer of Muslim background can discover that their life structure, which is so prescribed in Islam, need not suddenly lose all the pattern that it once had. They can try the ancient paths and disciplines that Christians have practiced for two thousand years and which still help us today to continue being disciples in effective, fruitful and relevant ways.

Spiritual disciples are not just taught but caught. Judi remembers her surprise when one lady she was mentoring told her how she was helping another in turn. "I remembered what you did with me and just did the same with her," she said. Of course it is important to remember that every person is unique, learns differently and has different questions. Therefore you will vary how you explain the biblical principles of why to do a spiritual discipline, how you structure the time you spend together doing the activity and how you encourage them to keep going. Different people will warm to some disciplines more than others so it doesn't help to push something that the person may not be ready for yet.

---

25 John 14:21, Romans 12:1.

26 James 1: 22.

27 Two excellent books which engage more fully on this whole topic are "The Spirit of the Disciplines" by Dallas Willard and "Spiritual Disciplines for the Christian Life" by Donald S Witney. Reading either of these books sets this brief chapter into a fuller perspective and would be really useful to discuss together with a believer from a Muslim background.

Lifestyle disciplines

As well as 'spiritual' disciplines, let's also think about 'lifestyle' disciplines. What gives our lives structure are the daily routines of family, work, social and religious life, even the personal routines of washing and dressing, eating and relating to others. All these are tied together in our world view. When this is disrupted, as in the case of a change of faith, it leaves a huge hole in our lives. If a new believer also has to move away from home the change will be all the greater. They may have to fend for themselves in ways they have never done before. If they previously had a sheltered life they may need to learn how to go shopping, how to cook, how to manage a budget or repair things around the house. Or if still living at home they may sense discomfort because the new perspective on life clashes with what is heard from those around. If the family know the BMB is now a Christian there may be active aggression.

Every family, whatever the faith background, provides structure through its daily routines and what role is expected of its members. Muslims know their place within the family and community and what their duties are towards the different members. With their new faith, they have to own responsibility rather than relying on habit, duty, shaming or coercion - ways they may have experienced before. As we keep reiterating, such freedom is hard and all areas of life will be affected by being a Christian; finances, career, intellect, self-care, health, family, emotional, spiritual and marriage.

Not all believers may want or need practical help in these areas, but how practically do we help if needed? One way is to have a plan and be ready! A coordinated plan will help to create a new norm as well as build the foundations for maturity. While recognising that a plan is a framework to flex from, not a rigid system which must be adhered to, here are some suggestions for how the Christian community can help new believers and how believers can help themselves.

The responsibility of the church

First, be ready to provide one person or family to mentor, visit, provide hospitality, phone or text etc. on a daily basis. In the first weeks and months this mentor should go gently with basic kindness, warmth, love, settling in, visits out together, and asking the new believer to join you in whatever you are doing if appropriate. They may take time to find out their new friend's story and likes and dislikes, including and dietary constraints.

Over the first few weeks and months help to establish a new practical daily and weekly routine based on new spiritual disciplines, spending time with the new family, and appropriate church activities. A structured timetable to the day is important whether the believer is in employment or not.

Secondly, have a small team of people ready to be involved in supporting the main mentor/family but also ready to befriend the BMB and share the work of supporting. Try to get together a group who are willing to be texted, phoned, and called on; who will also offer hospitality, help with signposting according to their gifting, and be willing to be 'close family' for that person.

Thirdly, the wider Church family can help by being welcoming; inviting the new person to join a house group, youth group, or prayer group as relevant; help them to feel welcome and included even if they don't want to take up the invitation. As time goes on another step is to give responsibility such as joining one of the rotas at Church such as tea and coffee, flowers, cooking, cleaning, worship - and hosting the study group, according to training, ability and gifting. We are doing more than just being friendly - this contributes to building a new pattern of activities and structure into life.

The responsibility of the new believer

Building a new ordered lifestyle is also the responsibility of the BMB which grows and develops over time. We asked one friend what she had found most helpful when she had had to leave home because her family could not accept her faith decision. Her first response was the love and help she received from her Christian friends, but in terms of her own responsibility she said two things were important.

The first was to have an aim, a purpose. She personally decided she wanted to further her education and enrolled on a degree course. She wanted to grow in her love for God, but having an aim gave her a purpose and a structure to her life. The second and most important thing was to set good boundaries. As a Muslim woman, in order to maintain her own and her family's honour, she had always dressed modestly, was home by ten o'clock at night, was careful not to be seen on her own with men and obeyed food laws. She realised that these things had given her self-respect and although as a Christian she did not have to obey dress or food rules, she felt she wanted to continue with them so she could hold her head high within the Muslim community whatever they said about her. She felt they would keep the door open into the community if people couldn't criticise her for staying out all night clubbing, having boyfriends and eating pork. Setting these boundaries helped her maintained her self-respect and integrity in dealings with the very minimal family contact she had.

She wanted to be with people she could trust and feel 'safe' with. Although she was introduced to many new friends she made her own judgements about who to spend the majority of her time with. With some she made her own boundaries about what topics to discuss with them, what invitations to accept and how much time to spend with them. She created a new mental list of those she felt she had a 'duty' towards, showing her appreciation to them by cooking and giving gifts.

It is helpful to discuss boundaries with our new friends, showing respect for their choices, supporting them as they struggle to get into new routines, thinking about their educational and skill development if that is what is important to them. BMBs usually maintain a bit of contact with someone in their family, maybe a sibling or cousin, and this is discussed further in Chapter 9.

Intentional change

We all struggle with changing habits, especially if we don't have accountability - just think about dieting! It may help for a mentor and a BMB to work together in a framework which gives this accountability. We offer one model in Appendix 3, and here briefly is another called 'the ABC model':

- A is for Aspiration - what do I want to be;
- B is for Behaviour - the things necessary to help this become a reality;
- C is for Choices - things I need to do to make changes in my behavior.

For example:

ASPIRATION	BEHAVIOURS	CHOICES
Be Reliable	Punctuality (on time for work)	1. Disciplined evening routine so I go to bed on time
		2. Disciplined morning routine - get up when the alarm goes off
	Integrity	3. Be honest when I am late

(Tim writing…)

Summary

In this chapter we looked at why the loss of an ordered life structure is often an issue for those leaving Islam, and at biblical principles which can guide a new framework in Christ. Biblical principles also help in evaluating what from one's own culture can be retained (enriching Christ's community in the process), what can be reinterpreted and what should be rejected. We considering practical ways of developing a good life structure, in relation to both 'spiritual disciplines' and 'lifestyle disciplines'. These are no guarantee of success but a useful framework. Ultimately your friend must be led by God's Spirit in these things. But be aware that the lack of specific guidelines in Christianity, along with our secular culture in the West, make it a challenge for them to build new life-structures in place of the Islamic ones. They may appreciate your help in this, on their road to the ultimate goal of maturity in Christ.

POINTS TO PONDER:

1 What points in this chapter had you never thought about before?

2 Many but not all Christians of Muslim background find the loss of ordered lifestyle to be a problem. Have you talked to your own BMB friend about it, and what do they say?

3 If your BMB friend asks you, "What are the rules for praying as a Christian?" how will you reply? Will you say, "There are no rules, just do what you like, just pray whenever it comes into your head"? Or will you give them a whole new set of fixed prayers to say at fixed times in a fixed way? Or will you suggest some middle way? What principles underlie your preferred approach?

4 Your friend is unsure whether they should join their still-Muslim family in fasting during Ramadan? How could you help them approach this question?

Joining the Family

CHAPTER NINE

Continuing relationship with birth community

(Roxy writing…)

Imagine your daughter, whom you love and have brought up to be a good Christian person, has just told you that she is now not a Christian but has decided to follow Islam. You feel shocked and betrayed in some ways because you never thought it possible. What she, as a new believer, thinks is exciting and amazing, is for you one of the worst days of your life. What do you do? How do you respond to this news?

I am reminded of the advice the character Atticus Finch offers to his daughter, Scout, in *To Kill a Mockingbird*. He said we will never really understand a person until we've considered things from his point of view; "until you climb into his skin and walk around in it."[1] In thinking about the pain which BMBs feel when their loved ones reject them, we should also "climb into the skin" of those family members and understand the pain they too feel when their son, daughter, brother or sister leaves the faith in which they were nurtured.

How and when to tell family you are a follower of Jesus?

I told my family quite soon after I came to faith, which turned out to be bad judgment on my part due to the fact that my relationship with them had already been difficult for various reasons. I told them at a time when their perception of Christians was based on misconceptions and what they saw on TV. They believed Christians were people who slept around, got drunk and were immoral; I found that it was difficult for them to think of Christians as anything else. They believed I'd joined the ranks of the immoral white people. I didn't have the opportunity to challenge these misconceptions even if I'd wanted to as they were very angry

---

1   Harper Lee, *To Kill A Mockingbird*, (Arrow, 2010), p.33

with me, as was the rest of the community. And if I'm honest the feeling was mutual, I was angry with them and with Muslims in general. I didn't want anything to do with Muslims and especially with Pakistani people. I felt betrayed by them and I felt I couldn't trust them. I found the culture and the religion oppressive and controlling.

This meant that any continued contact with my family and community was full of tension and conflict, so I kept my distance from them for at least six years. At the same time, I needed time to grow in my faith and to come to terms with my roots, my Pakistani-ness. I threw myself into life in the Christian community, which involved building new friendships, helping to run the youth club on a Monday evening, going to church twice on a Sunday and attending a youth group after church on a Sunday. I made some very deep friendships at that time and I started to understand more about redemption, forgiveness and reconciliation. I started to understand that I needed to think about my own attitude and response towards the people in the community I grew up in. I started to realise that God expected me to be like him, a God who forgives, who loves and is full of grace and I felt challenged to try and find a way to reconcile with my family and community.

Steve Bell, national director of Interserve England and Wales, comments:

The first believer that I walked with in Egypt took his vocabulary from a Western radio programme and told his family that he had 'become a Christian' - which was unnecessary. But these difficulties had kicked off before we met. So I was trying to help him pick up the pieces with a family that was irate, because they perceived betrayal of what it means to be Egyptian, to be part of that family, what it means to be a Muslim.[2]

Steve's comment that it was unnecessary for this former Muslim to describe himself as a Christian is an important point about how to tell family. Given the connotations of the word 'Christian' with the history of violence between people of the two faith groups, it might be better for a BMB to explain that they have become a follower of Jesus.

Useful insights about telling family

When a new believer is at the beginning of their journey there is excitement and joy; there is enthusiasm and therefore a desire to share what has happened, as they have met Jesus and have decided to follow Him. But there will also be difficult decisions to make about when and how to tell their family.

Since this decision can have an impact on the relationship with their family for a long time to come, it needs a lot of consideration. Yet often Western Christians don't realise what a critically important issue this is for BMBs, so they do nothing to

---

2 *Joining the Family* course

help the new believer think it through. Tom Walsh in his research on discipleship of believers of Muslim background, found that three-quarters of his interviewees had been given no advice at all from their Christian mentors, and the rest had received very little:

Tom Walsh
When family is so important to an MBB it is difficult to understand this silence. Surely the very thing which is uppermost on the part of the new believer, the family, should at least be taken seriously by those entrusted to nurture them?[3]

This chapter draws together some insights that may help you as you seek to support Christ's followers in relating to their Muslim families, remembering always that they need to make their own decisions and should not be pressured in any way by you or other believers. So here are some thoughts:

- There's no rush for the BMB to tell their family, it's good to give them time to grow in their faith first. As Joseph an Arab BMB said, "Build up your faith first".[4] Having said that, sometimes when it's left too long it can be more difficult to broach the subject.

- Some believers may never want to tell their family. It's important that they are allowed to make their own choice about this, especially as the repercussions will affect them and their relationship with those they love.

- Therefore believers need God's help, wisdom and guidance to know when to tell the family. Favour a BMB from Nigeria says, "Depend on God." Ask him to show you the right time. "At the right time God will link you up."[5]

- Every family situation is different, therefore responses will vary; so be prepared for many possible reactions: some positive and some difficult. Sometimes family members will never be able to accept the decision that the BMB has made, and will always feel betrayed.

- After reading Tom Walsh's research and listening to BMBs it seems that the longer a family lives with the new believer and sees the change in them before they are told the more likely they are to accept them in the family still. Steve Bell mentioned the father of an Iranian dental student who said, "We don't like what you've done, but we like what you've become, just don't

---

3   Thomas J. Walsh, 'Voices from Christians in Britain with a Muslim background: Stories for the British church on evangelism, conversion, integration and discipleship', MA dissertation, (University of Wales, 2005), p.35.
4   *Joining the Family* course.
5   *Joining the Family* course.

tell the wider family, don't disgrace us. We like what we see. You are a better son since you started following Jesus."[6]

- Where BMBs have had a good relationship with their family before conversion, it's vital for them to keep contact open if the relationship is to continue. Bear in mind though that some believers may need to have a time away from family for their own safety.

- Mubashir, a Pakistani BMB says, "I advise them to try not to rebel from their homes; try to show such an attitude that they don't oppose you. And living with them, give the gospel of Christ through your attitude, your character and your good deeds, share Christ in those ways. When you convert, they themselves will feel (…) 'This is not like the person he was before'(…) Don't give them any cause for opposing you, but live with them until such time comes that you're forced to leave".[7]

- When the BMB does decide to tell their family, it's good to be praying for them and the family too: before, during and after.

- Pray for wisdom for the right words. Talk with the BMB beforehand about what language they are going to use to describe the decision they have made. Certain words can have baggage attached to them. For instance, the word 'Christian' has connotations that the BMB has now become a traitor, sleeps around, drinks alcohol and eats pork. Describing oneself as a follower of Jesus can be better. It may be that by the time that the believer from a Muslim background tells his family, they already recognise this to be the case as they've seen changes in his/her behavior and character. Therefore this is not a shock to them but a recognition of the truth. Ultimately this decision needs to be made by the BMB themselves and thought through with your help.

- It's good to allow the family some time to process what they have been told. It's best not to assume from their first response that they will want to make life difficult for their family member. After the initial reaction they may ask him/her not to tell anyone else or they may just need some time to get used to what this means for them and the relationships in the community. Giving them this time is respectful and honours them and is important for the ongoing relationship. It also shows sensitivity to them knowing that this is inevitably difficult for them.

6   *Joining the Family* course.
7   Cited in Tim Green's PhD thesis, 'Issues of Identity for Christians of a Muslim Background in Pakistan', (London University, 2014).

- If you are discipling a BMB it may be good for you to get to know the family – maybe even before they make a decision to follow Christ, especially for younger people. My friends shared about a situation where they knew a lad of about 18 who came to faith. They said at first they didn't get to know the family of the boy and received threatening phone calls from them. But then when they invited his mother to tea and she got to know them she was a lot happier about her son's decision. The family may be helped by seeing that their child is spending time with godly people in a decent community.

In some circumstances, after the family find out the believer from a Muslim background may need to leave the family and community. In that case they will need you and their church family to support, by helping them find a safe place to stay and people to talk to about the pain and shock of the situation. They will need time to be with God and people who will help to comfort them at this time of grief.

Iranian believers are in a unique situation today, in that many are coming to faith and many seem open to Christianity due to what God is doing at this time, and also due to the form of Shia Islam they have been forced to live under and are willingly rejecting. Their method of disclosing their new-found faith to their family is more direct; they are aware of the prevalent hunger for something different to Shia Islam amongst Iranians and they realise that their decision will at least be understood.

Reza (Iranian BMB)

I told my dad in a very straightforward way, I told him, "I've found Christ, he's the true way, this is the encounter I've had with him". He laughed at me and rejected me for six months. When he saw the changes in me he started to read the Bible and do some research. We prayed for him and after nine years he surrendered to Jesus.[8]

Many Iranian believers would say that because there's a revival going on amongst Iranians, these days it's wisest to just call family directly and preach the gospel to them. They report that preaching directly, sharing the gospel, introducing Jesus as Son of God is very effective. Some families, however, are defensive and reject it at first. Then after two or three weeks they are the ones who come back and ask questions and ask for a Bible. They may have had a dream or vision in this time. It's helpful to remember that some Iranian families are devout Muslims, maybe with members of the family in positions of religious authority. It is very different telling them from telling a more secular Muslim family.

8   *Joining the Family* course.

Dealing with persecution

I had a Christian friend say to me: "Believers from Muslim background shouldn't be afraid of persecution, in fact they should expect it as it will strengthen their faith and honour God." I find it difficult to agree with this argument, considering that this was coming from a Westerner who hadn't had to sacrifice much at all in order to follow Jesus and had never suffered persecution. This is partly because of imbalanced teaching in the church. Time and again we are told that persecution is always good for Christians and church growth. But sometimes it isn't! And we are definitely not to seek persecution for its own sake.

We might have put our neck out for our faith in school, at work or even with non – Christian family or friends but none of us looks for persecution and suffering, and none of us would believe that our loving heavenly Father would will suffering for our lives. We believe that God isn't cruel and doesn't enjoy making us suffer but he can, and does, use persecution to bring about good in our lives and to help us mature.

For many BMBs it is very likely that at some point on their journey they will suffer persecution from family and community. For some it is the *words* of family members such as 'traitor' and 'apostate' and 'deserter' that cause pain. For others there may be *emotional blackmail*, such as being told that it is their fault if a family member becomes ill or dies, and or that the whole family is dishonoured before the community because of the decisions the BMB has made. For my friend, Saima, and others like her who choose to stay within the family home there may be *humiliating treatment* such as being forced to sleep on the floor or in the kitchen, or being told she can't eat with the rest of the family. They suffer threats of physical violence. Many are *disowned* by family and treated as if they are dead with no contact from the family at all. For others there may be *physical violence*, beatings, kicking's, and even death.

In all these circumstances it's important to remember it takes a great amount of determination and courage to continue in faith in Jesus. In these circumstances BMBs need support and understanding from others believers. We need great wisdom to support them in discerning the right path.

My own experience is that persecution has come to me in many forms: including friends cutting off all contact with me and disowning me, being threatened by community members and told that I was a traitor, being told I needed to go back to Islam or my mother would die and it would be my fault. And so on…

My response to this persecution was to believe more determinedly in Jesus and to trust Him with my life; I asked believers around me to help me and support me in prayer and they even provided a place where I could live safely. Words from the Bible comforted me and I saw God provide for me so generously, giving me people who loved and accepted me into their family. I learned that Jesus keeps his promises. His response to those who do have to leave everything behind makes me think he believed it would happen to his followers after his resurrection:

And everyone who has left houses or brothers or sisters or father or mother or wife or children or fields for my sake will receive a hundred times as much and will inherit eternal life.[9]

Ongoing relationship with family

For Christ's love compels us, because we are convinced that one died for all, and therefore all died. And he died for all, that those who live should no longer live for themselves but for him who died for them and was raised again. So from now on we regard no one from a worldly point of view. Though we once regarded Christ in this way, we do so no longer. Therefore if anyone is in Christ, the new creation has come, the old has gone, the new is here! All this is from God, who reconciled us to himself through Christ and gave us the ministry of reconciliation.[10]

Over a period of several years, I attempted three or four times to reconcile with my family, I tried rebuilding our relationship by moving closer to them so that I could spend more time with them. I opened my heart to them and shared my faith with them. I was given the opportunity to share with them what it meant to follow Christ. I spent time with all of the members of my family but I felt like a stranger - a foreigner in their midst.

I felt like I had changed so much that I couldn't feel comfortable in the community; I was aware of being observed every minute I was around them. Each of the three or four attempts would end in the tension between us rising and their expectations of me remaining unchanged - that I would go back to Islam, that I would move back home and get married to a person they chose for me. When I refused they would get aggressive, so I would need to cut off all contact with them again which broke my heart over and over again.

After ten years I came to realise that no matter what I did, their expectations of me would not change, and that I had done all I could to reconcile with them. I had to let go of them and of any hope of restoring our relationship, and so I was finally able to grieve the loss of my family. This meant that when I did have contact with any of my family I was free to enjoy the time but I didn't leave a part of me behind. It was much easier to relax and enjoy whatever the relationship was to become with no expectations. By this point I had met my husband and married and I had a very close Christian family where I belonged. Though I grieved the loss of my biological family God had given me a new family and I was so grateful! Though there are still times when I feel the pain of not sharing life with my biological family.

Throughout this time my Christian friends didn't know what advise to give

9   Mathew 19:29, NIV.
10 2 Corinthians 5:13-18, NIV.

me on how I should relate to my family or community. On one hand, many of them never broached the subject in conversation. But on the other hand, when someone did ask me how things were going, I'd feel guilty and thought that I should do more to keep the connection with my family. How do I "honour my parents", as the commandment says, in this situation? I didn't know how to put this commandment into practice. As a very young teenage girl I didn't really understand my own feelings enough to be able to explain how I felt to my friends. Most of my Christian friends knew that my relationship with my parents was complicated and not without pain, but they didn't know how I felt and what had really happened between my parents and me.

What really helped me at this time is that these Christians were prepared to accept me into their own homes and share some of their own family times with me without expectations of me. The question of whether I should share my faith and pray for my family to come to faith was left unsaid. Perhaps harder to bear, over the years whenever I've shared my story, was when people who didn't know me said things like "Do you still see your family?" "How is your relationship with your family?" "Should I pray for your family to come to know Jesus?" All these questions were said out of love and curiosity, but they often left me feeling guilty and ashamed about my relationship with my family. I'm used to these questions now and sometimes I am bold enough to say, "I'm sorry, I don't want to share that with you", which most people do accept. Kind questions can be difficult. I think if you hear a believer share their testimony or speak of coming from a Muslim background, and you don't know them well, it is wise to think before you ask them questions. What's the reason you're asking the question and how will it make them feel?

However, if you are in a friendship and walking alongside the BMB it's a different story. There are times when the subject of family comes up naturally and then it's helpful that you ask how the relationship is going, that is a sign of the strength of the relationship you have. But it's important that this is done by one or two close people and comes out of relationship rather than from people who don't know the believer well. Don't forget that asking about family is a sensitive question.

I realise that this is my experience, and other believers of Muslim background will have their own unique experiences. Many have been reconciled to members of their families and many have seen their families come to faith since their own conversion. Javed, an Afghan BMB, talks about his relationship with his family and how he found reconciliation with them over time:

Javed

I think that's one of the most difficult challenges that most new believers face. Most of my family is now aware that I have come to Christ. And it is quite challenging because of the misconceptions they have about the Christian faith, especially my sisters-in-law and my in-laws' family, I had trouble with them in the beginning, so they didn't contact me. But these issues can be resolved over time, they came to some kind of understanding that we have come to Christ. But it takes time. And we need to be wise and pray to God. The Holy Spirit will tell us the right time to speak to our families - when they are ready to hear.[11]

When Favour, a BMB, first told her father that she had become a Christian he said, "I disown you, stop using my name, leave my house." But over the years, as she sought to restore the relationship with her family, the Holy Spirit showed her how to honour her parents. She has loved them and now after twenty years she describes her relationship with her father as "awesome". She is able to pray with her father, on the phone, in Jesus' name!

The reality is that the relationship between the believer from Muslim background and their family will change in some way, a change influenced by the BMB's choice to follow Jesus. In part, this change is inevitable because the BMB will be a new person - becoming a follower of Jesus means we will be transformed and changed to be more like him. Also the change of faith for one person within the family will mean the rest of the family will have to adapt the way they relate to him/her; they may now not be able to share their religious beliefs - that very important aspect of their life - the way they used to. They will need to relearn how to relate and make the relationship possible which may take a long time. It all depends, of course, on how the family responds to the believer's new faith and how the believer is able to respond to his/her family.

According to Rasheeda, some Christians just assumed that her family ill-treated her because she became a believer and therefore they were awful people. This stereotypical image that we have of how Muslim families will treat those who convert isn't helpful to the BMB, as it puts pressure on them to prove their family are good people who love them too. It's best to remember that each situation and family is unique and will have a different response.

Long-term outcomes

To summarise, there can be different long-term outcomes in the relationship with family:

- ongoing coldness in the relationship
- active hostility where the family pursues the BMB to bring them back or even kill them
- reconciliation with family but they don't turn to Christ, as with Favour and her father
- reconciliation and some turn to Christ, as with Reza and his father
- total estrangement from family and community.

---

11 *Joining the Family* course

Forgiveness and reconciliation

Understanding the principles of Jesus' teaching about forgiveness and reconciliation is vital for BMBs in their relationship with family and with God. Here are some of them:

> For if you forgive other people when they sin against you, your heavenly Father will also forgive you.[12]

> Then Peter came to Jesus and asked, "Lord, how many times shall I forgive my brother or sister who sins against me? Up to seven times?" Jesus answered, "I tell you, not seven times, but seventy-seven times".[13]

The people who modeled this to me the most were my Christian family and friends. They shared about the difficult relationships in their lives and the times they needed to ask for forgiveness in order to reconcile with others.

One of the most challenging lessons I have learned was when there was a difference in opinion with Christians who were there to support me, and we had to work together through to a place of forgiveness and reconciliation. My friends were considering sharing information with a local government office that I felt would risk my security, and this gave me many sleepless nights. Eventually we came to a place of forgiveness after understanding their reasons for wanting to share this information. We were able to reconcile and move on, and our relationship is stronger than ever before. I learned from them and from the situation that keeping communication going between you, even when it's painful, can help the relationship in the long run. As well as being honest about the situation and its consequences for me I was able to recognise the dilemma and difficulty it caused them and we were able to move on. I saw and felt God's love in and through them.

> If your brother or sister sins, go and point out their fault, just between the two of you. If they listen to you, you have won them over. But if they will not listen, take one or two others along, so that "every matter may be established by the testimony of two or three witnesses." If they still refuse to listen, tell it to the church; and if they refuse to listen even to the church, treat them as you would a pagan or a tax collector.[14]

This is just as true in the relationship between BMBs and their birth family. Sadly sometimes it's not possible to reconcile with the person who has wronged you, but there is still a need to forgive the family. When a person isn't able to forgive, the result is often bitterness and depression that they carry through life. For some people this journey towards being able to forgive the family takes time. If we don't

---

12 Matthew 6:14, NIV.
13 Matthew 18:21-22, NIV.
14 Matthew 18: 15-17, NIV.

forgive, reconciliation is less likely. Unforgiveness leads to bitterness that eats away at us and has power over us until we decide to let go and forgive - this is a choice that we may need to make over and over again.

Corrie Ten Boom
Forgiveness is the key that unlocks the door of resentment and the handcuffs of hatred. It is a power that breaks the chains of bitterness and the shackles of selfishness.[15]

I am amazed at the capacity God gives me to forgive my family, because I never thought I would be able to forgive them. Forgiveness needs to happen even when reconciliation isn't possible. They may never acknowledge the hurt they have caused me, but by forgiving them I'm releasing myself from them, and I'm also allowing God to be the one who deals with their sin. I'm saying, "I forgive them, Father, and I'm trusting that you'll do the rest". We need to allow the BMB to make that journey towards being able to forgive, and to pray for them in this difficult decision without judgement and condemnation. BMBs may also need to ask for forgiveness for the hurt they may have caused their family members. God will work in their hearts as they walk in obedience to him, and he will show them what they need to do to reconcile with family.

BMBs sharing faith with their Muslim family and community
Earlier we looked at what happens when BMBs reveal to family that they themselves follow Christ. A separate question is when and how they invite their relatives to follow Christ too.

Once, when I was able to visit my family, my younger sister began to ask me questions about the differences between Islam and Christianity, and what I believed about Jesus and why I believed it. This gave me my first opportunity to share openly with them, my mum, sisters, nephew and niece, about my faith in Jesus and his love for them. I felt the presence of God with me giving me the words to speak. On another occasion, my mum was sharing the story of Yousef (Joseph) with me; she couldn't remember part of it and I finished telling her the story. She asked me how I knew the story of Yousef (Joseph), and I said to her, "It's in the Bible as well as the Qur'an". Her response was surprise and a smile. "What do you think it means?" she asked. I said, "It means that we can be reconciled to each other if we allow God to guide us and are not stubborn". Again she was surprised and smiled. Those were my two opportunities to share my faith with family members and I felt delighted that God had given me those opportunities and the words to speak. They may not have come to know Jesus for themselves but we were further down the line, both in understanding each other and in their awareness of some of the misconceptions they had about Jesus and Christian belief.

---

15 Corrie Ten Boom, *Clippings from my notebook*, (Thomas Nelson, 1982).

Others' experiences

Different believers of Muslim background share their faith with their Muslim families in different ways:

Khalad Hussain (British Pakistani)

When I go and visit my family, in the UK or in Pakistan, I don't have any Christian literature with me. It would not be safe to use overt Christian language and yet I know I can share my faith with them. I am conscious that I may be the only bit of the Bible they are reading that day. More than anywhere, in such situations, I am conscious of being an ambassador of Christ.[16]

Asghar (from Iran)

I want to give God's present to everyone… including Iranians.[17]

Reza (also from Iran)

Witnessing to the Iranian community is very straightforward. When I first meet the individual I ask them about their life: are they satisfied with Islam, do they know Jesus? I tell them who Jesus is and then they start sharing about their life. I say, "For all these years there has been a veil around your eyes and head about Jesus. Jesus is not just a prophet, he's the Son of God. There's a Bible in Farsi, would you like to read the Bible?" I will push the gospel. Then they start to ask questions. They will talk about the deep desire they have to know God. 50% of the time they become Christians the first time. God has softened their hearts. And often they are running away from something; when they are willing to experience Jesus they will find out that he's the one who can help them with their pain. As soon as they start trusting Jesus, God shows up. We use book-tables to draw Iranians into conversation and often Iranians invite each other to conferences; here also a seed of God is sown.[18]

The Church's relationship with the Muslim community

It can be helpful if there is a connection between the Muslim and Christian community before a Muslim person from that community becomes a believer. I have heard of instances when the church and mosque leaders already met regularly and had a good relationship of mutual respect and trust. Then, when a Muslim person has come to believe in Jesus as Lord and Saviour, the church and mosque leaders have helped the family to come to terms with the decision. In addition, their previous discussions about what it means to be a Christian and

---

16 Khalad Hussain, *Against the Grain*, (Xlibris, 2012), p. 174.
17 *Joining the Family* course.
18 Personal communication.

their existing trusting relationship has enabled the mosque leader to understand more deeply what being a believer is about. They can advise the family to be more open and keep the relationship with the new believer open and loving, where the family may have been tempted to reject the new believer because of their lack of understanding about Christianity. I am also aware that there is a cost to both leaders as their congregation members may not like this relationship that they have, and may accuse them of being too friendly with people from another religion. Often this sort of relationship takes years to build and is a result of activities in the church building such as mother and toddlers groups, after school clubs and youth clubs which have been attended by Muslim children. Where the church provides other helpful services, such as clinics, accessed by the Muslim community, fears and unfounded perceptions can be broken down.

Conclusion

In conclusion, it's important for a BMB to be able to have some sort of relationship with their birth family and community where possible. As you've read, they need a lot of wisdom and guidance from God and they need us to support them in these decisions without judgment or pressure. God can do what seems impossible, and many families do come to faith in Jesus as Reza's did. But others don't, and that is very painful for the one who is following Jesus. You've read how the church can play a part in witnessing to Muslims, and we have much to learn from believers of Muslim background who are courageous in witness and share the gospel even when they risk persecution.

POINTS TO PONDER:

1 What would you feel if a family member became a Muslim? How would this affect that person's relationships with your family?

2 After reading this chapter, how will you support BMBs in their relationships with family members?

3 Bearing in mind that Christians' positive relationship with the Muslim community can make it easier for those who convert, how will you encourage the church to become more involved with Muslims in your area?

Joining the Family

CHAPTER TEN

Especially for church leaders

(Roxy writing…)

A church leader's role in the Bible and in churches today

The Bible describes the church using word-pictures, such as the church as a body[1] and as the branches of a vine.[2] The body has many parts which all work together to get things done. They rely on each other. Jesus is the vine and the church is the branches. One of several possible interpretations is that the church should do the good things that Jesus asks them to do, following the example he set us. So, just as Jesus loved people, the Church should be a place where all people will find love and support. The Church is also described as a priesthood of believers.[3] In Biblical times Jewish priests were chosen by God to help people in the community to get to know him better: by speaking his words to them, praying for them and helping them experience his love and forgiveness for themselves.

The Church of England Liturgy of Ordination puts it like this:

> Priests are called to be servants and shepherds among the people to whom they are sent. With their Bishop and fellow ministers, they are to proclaim the word of the Lord and to watch for the signs of God's new creation. They are to be messengers, watchmen and stewards of the Lord; they are to teach and to admonish, to feed and provide for his family, to search for his children in the wilderness of this world's temptations, and to guide them through its confusions, that they may

---

1   Ephesians 1:22-23.
2   John 15.
3   1 Peter 2:9.

be saved through Christ forever. Formed by the word, they are to call their hearers to repentance and to declare in Christ's name the absolution and forgiveness of their sins.

With all God's people, they are to tell the story of God's love. They are to baptise new disciples in the name of the Father, and of the Son, and of the Holy Spirit, and to walk with them in the way of Christ, nurturing them in the faith. They are to unfold the Scriptures, to preach the word in season and out of season, and to declare the mighty acts of God. They are to preside at the Lord's table and lead his people in worship, offering with them a spiritual sacrifice of praise and thanksgiving. They are to bless the people in God's name. They are to resist evil, support the weak, defend the poor, and intercede for all in need. They are to minister to the sick and prepare the dying for their death. Guided by the Spirit, they are to discern and foster the gifts of all God's people, that the whole Church may be built up in unity and faith.[4]

The Methodist Worship Book puts it simply as:

In God's name you are to preach by word and deed the Gospel of God's grace; to declare God's forgiveness of sins to all who are penitent; to baptize, to confirm and to preside at the celebration of the sacrament of Christ's body and blood; to lead God's people in worship, prayer and service; to minister Christ's love and compassion; to serve others, in whom you serve the Lord himself. These things are your common duty and delight. In them you are to watch over one another in love.[5]

Thus the role of a leader in the church is one of servanthood and sacrifice and is often felt to be a calling rather than a career. It is a calling that is at times very difficult but also very rewarding as you see many grow in faith and in intimacy with Christ Jesus. You have the privilege of sharing in people's joys and sorrows, at baptisms, weddings and funerals; you have a front row seat in the lives of the people you serve. It's a role that many of you do so well and I want to thank you for that at the beginning of this chapter. I am writing this chapter to you, not because you are not doing the things you should be doing, but because I want to encourage you and invite you to do these things even better with more knowledge and hopefully helpful understanding of the unique situation of BMBs in your congregation.

---

4   https://www.churchofengland.org/prayer-worship/worship/texts/ordinal/priests.aspx
5   http://www.methodist.org.uk/media/1765496/called-to-ordained-ministry-0715.pdf

A church leader's role in discipleship of a believer of Muslim background

Brian Houston (Hillsong Church)
The impact of leadership to make or break a church, an organization or even a home is profound, and I believe the huge majority of people want to be led and respond to leadership.[6]

Leaders have great influence in the lives of the people who follow them. And for BMBs that's even more the case. We have been taught through our lives as Muslims that leaders are the ones whom we should obey without question, and so we look to you to lead us. A good example of this is given by Phil, an Anglican vicar:

Phil Rawlings (church leader)
When I was fairly new into leading a church in Manchester, a convert was in the congregation and he came to me and said, "You are my father in God, my father would arrange my marriage, would you find me a wife?" To which my comment was two previous appointments and three years of theological training never prepared me for this! And I think if we are going to be serious in terms of people coming to Christ, particularly if they are single, we as leaders of the church are going to need to pick up on these issues.[7]

The situation Phil describes is a very good example of this sense of respect. You leaders have a place in our discipleship that others don't have, you command a respect in our eyes that others don't. And we look to you as God's voice to us.

As believers from Muslim background grow in faith and understanding of church there will hopefully be a change in our view of leadership too. For instance, when the leader is female there can be some problems with accepting her authority as a leader due to the fact that the majority of leaders in the Muslim community are men. BMBs have been used to men in leadership and often are not used to women in leadership positions. Our attitude towards women in leadership will hopefully change as we grow in faith and understanding of church.

Culturally, BMBs will have a mentality that you are the Father of the church, the tribal chief of the church. This is very different from the servant model of leadership that many church leaders are taught at theological college, therefore it can feel very uncomfortable.

---

6   http://www.philcooke.com/live-love-lead-an-interview-with-brian-houston
7   *Joining the Family* course.

Phil Rawlings (church leader)

Leaders need to understand that they have both a responsibility to help the BMB to integrate into the culture of the church which isn't one of deference and also that their behaviour as church leader is being watched and that the BMB will learn a lot more from watching how leaders behave than by listening to their sermons.[8]

We who are believers from a Muslim background need to learn to balance respect for you with the reality that none of us are perfect and that you are as human as we are. The church is the place where together we can grow more like Jesus, being the people he has called us to be. You can help us in many ways. First, and most importantly, keep on pointing us to Jesus, his word and to prayer, remind us of our own place in God's family and help us in every season to look to God for strength.

Your crucial role

A church leader plays a crucial role in the discipleship of BMBs in two main ways:

1) A church leader has to take responsibility for ensuring there is good discipleship for the BMB. They must see it not as a separate ministry in the church but a ministry within the church that they have some control over, even if they don't do the discipling themselves.

2) The leader needs to engage with the discipleship of BMBs and needs to show that he or she is right behind what's going on. You can do this in a number of ways:

   1. At least be aware of and understand what's going on in the church and its implications for the BMB and the church. Doing a course like *Friendship First* or *Encountering the World of Islam* will help the church leader gain a greater understanding of the issues. See also the 'Recommended Resources' in Appendix 1.
   2. Mentor and support disciplers of BMBs to ensure accountability. The leader must take a hands-on role even if she's not doing the discipling herself. This is a ministry of the church therefore the church or leadership must take ultimate responsibility for the growth of those who are part of the church – including BMBs.
   3. The leader can communicate to their whole congregation that discipling of BMBs is a whole church matter. Everyone has a role in the process, especially those in leadership roles.

Clearly teach us why we have rituals in the church, being transparent and honest

---

8   Personal interview.

with us about the things that are not from the Bible but have been developed by the church as tools to help us be disciples. Treat us as one of the community, no different from another family member in many ways, but also with unique needs as a result of where we've come from. Help us to learn the principles of Bible study, prayer and life as a disciple of Jesus, enabling us to think out our beliefs in conversation with you and others in small groups.

These are the things we look to you for but you may not do this for us directly, you may ask others to walk alongside us in these ways. You may decide that you will commit to doing this yourself. Your involvement and blessing of us and honouring of us in this way is really important to us and shows us that we are part of God's family. It is easier for a church to develop separate streams for BMBs rather than struggle to overcome the challenges of being truly inclusive.

Throughout my walk with God I've been discipled by many people, most of whom haven't been church leaders or vicars, instead they have been equipped and are overseen by leaders in the church. Unfortunately, the people who discipled me had other demands put on them by church leaders as well as family, work and life in general. One way you as a church leader can help is by releasing from other church commitments those who feel called to disciple BMBs, and by encouraging them to be equipped and trained as much as possible in this calling. You can provide them with accountability and people who can support them as they disciple the BMBs in the church.

Do you remember pastor Ian, who found that many Iranians and Afghans started coming into his church? He saw they needed pastoral care and discipleship. So he responded partly by discussing with the church leadership team how to free up some of his own time for this ministry, and partly by forming a group of church members who could give themselves to it more fully. He told us:

Ian Jones
We have eight people who were mums and dads, they are mostly retired people, because they are available in the day. One is a retired primary school teacher who was desperate to teach English. She said to me: "Ian, I want to use my skills to teach English", so I said "I think I've got something for you".[9]

One believer from a Muslim background told me she felt a desperate need to be baptised because she was not a true believer until that had happened. The reason for this was that the vicar in her church had refused to serve her communion because she was not baptised. Of course she felt she didn't belong. This will not be true in all churches but I have heard other BMBs say similar things which made them feel excluded from the church. If this is the practice of your church it needs to be very carefully explained, and you as leader need to recognise that it will be very hard indeed for the BMB to understand.

---

9   *Joining the Family* course.

On the other hand my own experience has been that church leaders have been very supportive and caring towards me. I have been part of a Methodist church where the minister of the church invited me to be part of the community, and involved me in the service in small but central ways, from serving coffee to speaking. I have also been part of an Anglican church where the vicar helped me to find accommodation and he also spent time answering my theological questions. Later I have been part of another bigger Anglican church where the vicar was a bit more distant but acknowledged me and knew my name whenever I saw him at church, and that was enough for me as he'd also been involved in releasing others to care for me. These experiences have been significant and have helped me to belong to the church and find identity in Christ. When the vicar released people into the role of supporting and caring for me it meant I was immediately included in the family and I felt valued and that I belonged.

Nigel, another vicar, talks about how his small Anglican church became family to a Pakistani man who asked to become a believer. He has now become part of the church and the members are like family to him. Nigel led by example and his welcome of the BMB influenced his church members. In their own beautiful way they also welcomed the BMB, as you can read here:

Nigel (vicar)

At Christmas the church wardens, all four of them, got together without saying anything to me, and they bought him a Christmas present, which might seem quite a simple thing, it might be seen as not very much at all. It's an everyday thing at Christmas, but it's not every day, if you've lost your entire family and your friends are all effectively new. So it's very important that the church is able, in its own style, to make some effort to genuinely care for the person going through this new phase in their life.

One particular older woman, he calls her 'Mum', which is on one level slightly cheeky, on another level it's really very affectionate. And the fact that you can have affection as well, that is important. For some people it's going to be very important. They are human beings who need that.[10]

Building a relationship with Muslim leaders

As a leader, you may also play a big role in connecting with the imam of the local Muslim community of which a BMB may still be part. If you and the imam have a relationship of trust and understanding, this may help the BMB. It may mean that the imam is able to help the family of the BMB to understand what has happened to their relative and why it's OK for the BMB to make the choice he or she has

---

10 *Joining the Family* course.

made (there's more about this in Chapter 12).

God is interested in relationships, and in our engagement with Muslims relationships have got to be a priority. Leaders need to make friends with Muslims and set an example to their congregation in this way. In many locations up and down the country Church leaders and Mosque leaders have been meeting in groups for meals and discussions about faith. The relationships that have been established are important in making life easier for those who decide to leave Islam to follow Jesus.

Also, pastors and imams can join together to make peace between communities that may otherwise be tense. Established relationships between the Church and the Mosque have lead to a joint commitment to *'Ethical Guidelines for Christian and Muslim Witness'* in the UK. These guidelines were written by Andrew Smith who is Director of Interfaith Relations for the Diocese of Birmingham. The document was slightly amended and then formally adopted by members of the Christian Muslim Forum and has been used as a guideline by many Christians who work amongst Muslims in the UK. The guidelines include these two important points in relation to conversion:

> **Point 9:** Whilst recognising that either community will naturally rejoice with and support those who have chosen to join them, we will be sensitive to the loss that others may feel.

> **Point 10:** Whilst we may feel hurt when someone we know and love chooses to leave our faith, we will respect their decision and will not force them to stay or harass them afterwards.[11]

Not all Muslims will agree with this. In Britain they have a range of opinions about whether Muslims should be allowed to leave Islam, as described in Appendix 2. Even those who acknowledge this freedom in principle may still find it difficult in practice, and may find it particularly difficult to persuade their community and the family involved. Those who do agree with it in theory will still find it painful in practice if any of their own family came to faith and chose to leave Islam - just as any one of us would feel if it were our own son or daughter.

When difficulties come up between the two communities, Church and Mosque leaders can then fall back on the relationship of trust they have built:

Phil Rawlings (church leader)
So we're talking to people with whom we have shared food and have been able to engage in a way where we have agreed to differ and walked away friends.[12]

---

11 www.christianmuslimforum.org/images/Ethical_Guidelines_for_Witnessv10.pdf
12 Personal interview.

Sharing testimony in church

There are also other ways that you can help us along the lines suggested by N.T. Wright:

> We honour and celebrate our complexity and our simplicity by continually doing five things. We tell stories. We act out rituals. We create beauty. We work in communities. We think out beliefs.[13]

Honour and celebrate our story, the beauty of God's work in our lives by treating our testimony with respect and only asking us to share it when we are ready and want to. For many believers of Muslim backgrounds sharing testimony in church is a 'rite of passage' in their new lives as believers. It can strengthen their faith if it's shared at the right time in the journey and dealt with sensitively and carefully by the leaders around them. It's important that you, as the leader they respect and hold in high regard, only ask them to share testimony when it's the right time, because they are likely to say 'yes' to sharing it whenever you ask, due to the way they see you as a leader. Therefore, before making the request, you need to give it prayerful consideration and hear wisdom from others including those closest to the BMB.

Once you've decided it's the right time for them to share their testimony there are some other issues that you need to think through. First, in what context are you going to ask them to share the testimony? For example, it's ideal if it's in the context of lots of people sharing their own story, like a church I attended who had a series of testimonies over a few weeks. This makes the BMB feel like part of the whole church, not as an unusual person on a pedestal but it also shows the value of the story he has. Therefore context is important in order to avoid making the BMB feel like a trophy- especially when it comes to the day that they share their testimony. Think carefully about how you introduce them in front of the group in your church.

Another issue is how you plan to publicise that the BMB is going to share his or her testimony. If it's on the church website please check that the BMB is happy for you to share this online. If it's on a sign outside the church, again please check with the BMB. The concern is about their security and whether they have told family and friends in the Muslim community about their new faith. Be aware of their safety and check with them first. Khalad Hussain talks about a time when he agreed to speak to a group of church leaders in a nearby town. He also organised an activity within his own church and wrote about it for the church newsletter. News of both these occasions ended up on the internet and were linked to Khalad's name. Thankfully, it has not had any harmful consequences. But there is still a need for extra precaution.

Never share the BMB's story in your own preaching – in your church or

---

13 N.T. Wright, *Simply Christian*, (SPCK Publishing, 2011), p.49.

anywhere else – without asking their permission. It is their story. And never mention their name in your preaching without their consent.

It is important that the BMB moves on from telling their story of conversion to being asked to share other things or take other roles. There is a danger that the new believer only feels valued for their conversion rather than their growing faith, gifts, service etc.

OTHER TIPS FOR CHURCH LEADERS

1 Be prepared to make lots of mistakes as you minister to believers of Muslim background but learn from these mistakes.

2 Never think you've got the final word on anything, as each BMB's situation and each individual is unique and therefore complex.

3 Remember that all leaders involved in this ministry are feeling their way through on these issues so you're not alone in feeling out of your depth. In the end God's grace overrules!!!

4 Be transparent and work with others to find answers - it's important to show honesty and respect, and not try to pretend you know what you're doing all the time.

5 It's vital that you learn what you can in order to understand the background of new believers from Islam. Going on a *Friendship First* or *Encountering the World of Islam* course will help you to understand more about BMBs.

6 It's also important to help the church understand more about BMBs. We especially recommend that your church run the *Joining the Family* course which is directly on this topic, and that you take part in it too. One advantage of the course is that participants learn first hand from believers of Muslim background interviewed on film (and also if possible with BMBs taking part in the learning group itself). Also, the discussion times and learning tasks help participants towards transformation, not just information.

7 It is worth having contact with Mahabba and Joining the Family and other networks or organisations where you can learn, ask advice and work together.

(Tim writing…)

Baptising a believer of Muslim background

Nigel (church leader)
We got to the point when he was baptised in our church. He was baptised by immersion, and it's the very first time in our 300 year history that had happened in St Anne's.[14]

Even a generation ago it was a rare thing indeed for a British pastor to baptise someone of Muslim background. But now it is much more commonplace. For me, it is always such a thrilling occasion. Sometimes I have stood on an English river bank for the baptism of a believer by immersion in open view of the assembled congregation and even of curious onlookers. Equally in Pakistan I have attended secret baptisms in bathtubs with only one or two present, and where the person getting baptised faced real danger if discovered. Knowing the potential cost, it brings a lump to my throat whenever this hymn is sung as part of their baptismal promise:

> *I have decided to follow Jesus,*
> *I have decided to follow Jesus,*
> *I have decided to follow Jesus,*
> *No turning back, no turning back.*
>
> *The world behind me, the cross before me*
> *The world behind me, the cross before me*
> *The world behind me, the cross before me*
> *No turning back, no turning back.*
>
> *Though none go with me, still I will follow,*
> *Though none go with me, still I will follow,*
> *Though none go with me, still I will follow,*
> *No turning back, no turning back.*

There are many ways to baptise someone who has turned to Christ from Islam, and we certainly don't want to interfere with your church tradition. But, in the particular case of BMBs, here are some aspects to bear in mind, which you might not have thought about before.

1) What does it mean for the individual getting baptised?
Baptism is an important step for any adult, and perhaps all the more so for those coming from a different religion as they declare allegiance to Christ and to his

---

14 *Joining the Family* course.

community. The symbolism of dying and rising with Jesus means a lot to BMBs. They are nailing their colours to the mast. It's a point of no return. In preparing the person for baptism, you might like to take them through Chapter 15 of the course Come Follow Me which is specifically written for those of Muslim background.

2) What does it mean for the person's family?

Their Muslim families and community will almost certainly see this step as a mark of betrayal. Muslim attitudes towards apostasy may be shifting a little in the West, at least among the leaders, as explained in Appendix 2. Nevertheless, the immediate Muslim family and wider relatives of the person taking baptism see it as a humiliating disgrace, and especially if this news gets spread in their community. Try to be aware of this and reduce the shock and shame for the family as far as possible. Therefore, in preparing a BMB for baptism, don't just think about the spiritual dimension but also the social implications.

3) What practical preparations may be helpful?

Discuss with the individual:

- **When is the right time for them to be baptised?** Usually God will show this to them by his Spirit, so don't rush the process; but when the time is right, don't hold back either. I have noticed that when BMBs repeatedly express a strong desire to be baptised it is usually evidence that God's Spirit is prompting them within.

- **How will their culture be affirmed?** I was once present at an Iranian's baptism in a British church with several other Iranians there too. Most of the service took place in English but the pastor had also asked the Iranians to lead everyone in one baptismal song in Farsi. It was a lovely touch. It has even been suggested that the person getting baptised could make their vows in their mother tongue, with translation; an idea to consider, at least.

- **Which people should be present at the baptism?** At least some close trusted friends should normally be present, but what about the wider church? Or even non-Christians? In many cases it would be disastrous or at least difficult for Muslim relatives to be present; but occasionally they are open-minded enough to attend, despite the pain in their hearts, and this could do something to connect 'birth family' with 'new family'. Don't push for this as the BMB herself or himself knows best how the family will react, or whether to tell them beforehand about the baptism.

- **How will the church celebrate afterwards?** If a small party with refreshments can be arranged, it can give a wonderful message to the newly baptised person: "Welcome to the family!"

- **Will photos be taken at the baptism and how will their spread be controlled?** These days, with digital photos and Facebook this is a very important question! Public spread of baptism photos may create difficulties to the believer and will certainly bring dishonour to their family. The most sensitive point is when the BMB is going under the water, ESPECIALLY if it is a male Baptising a female. Such photos should be strictly controlled, e.g. by permitting only one trusted cameraperson at this point. But group photos afterwards, of the newly baptised person with their Christian friends, are less sensitive.

- **What steps will be taken to guard the modesty of females getting baptised?** Try to see this from a Muslim cultural perspective. What does it look like for a lady to be held in the water by a man who's not her husband? Females baptising females is best if possible. Another sensitive point is in coming out of the water, when wet clinging clothes can compromise modesty; the solution is to have thicker clothes and someone with a towel ready to wrap around her as she emerges from the water. These sound like small points but they make a difference, as the following account demonstrates:

A sad outcome which could have been avoided

My wife Rachel and I were closely involved in the life of an Iranian lady who came to study in Britain. Shireen (not her real name) met Christians, started exploring the faith, turned to Christ and prepared for baptism by a local vicar. This was to take place by full immersion in the river. As our friend was walking down to the riverbank in her long white baptismal clothes, she told Rachel with a smile, "The last time I was dressed like this was on pilgrimage in Mecca".

We weren't in control of proceedings and nothing was said about cameras. Sure enough, when Shireen was in the water getting baptised by the vicar people were taking digital photos. We were worried but there was nothing we could do. Anyway, it was a wonderful occasion and she was so happy.

Two days later Shireen turned up on our doorstep in floods of tears. She was so upset she couldn't speak to start with.

"What happened?" we asked.
"My husband phoned from Iran. He says he is divorcing me."
"But why?"

"Someone showed him a picture on Facebook, of me being held in the arms of another man, in the water in full view of the public! Think of the shame! Especially as he is well known by the religious leaders!"

The divorce went ahead.

That's why we care about this issue.

Conclusion

(Roxy writing...)

As church leaders you may feel totally out of your depth and overwhelmed at times but you will make a difference in people's lives. Here's how Phil describes ministry to believers of Muslim background:

Phil Rawlings (church leader)

It is complex but it is immensely exciting and it's hugely rewarding. Spending time with BMBs utterly opens your minds to what God is doing. God is breaking into these situations and it's utterly fantastic (...) The BMBs interaction with church and leadership will change us and we've got to be ready to be changed.[15]

In conclusion, I want to again thank you for being obedient to God in the calling to serve his people, and to love those in the church and reflect Jesus Christ in who you are and what you do. Thank you to the many leaders who have welcomed BMBs in to the church and, without knowing, have made them and me feel part of God's family by their acknowledgment and their open and warm acceptance into the life of the church. We need you to continue to model this to the rest of the church.

---

15 Personal interview.

POINTS TO PONDER:

1 After reading this chapter what do you think is unique about the role that church leaders play in the discipleship of BMBs?

2 What will you do differently now you've read about baptism and what it means to BMBs?

3 How can you involve BMBs in the life of your church as a church leader?

CHAPTER ELEVEN

Welcoming asylum seekers in the Church

(Emily Bowerman writing…)

> You could actually see them from the train, those people trying to get through the fence and onto lorries and into the UK. I felt so angry at them. I mean, there was me who'd done everything the right way and there they were trying to sneak in illegally.

My Canadian friend was back for a short visit and had just returned from a week in France. She had recently faced the disappointment of being refused permission to remain in the UK when her job came to an end, in spite of a stable relationship, community of friends, and a strong sense of being at home here.

Everyone around the table nodded empathetically at her statement about 'those people' who she'd seen trying to 'sneak in illegally'. I looked around at the group of well-educated, bright and kind Christian women, enjoying brunch together on a Saturday morning, and wondered what to say in response.

Should I tell the group that everyone had a right to seek safety from persecution and that that didn't make them 'illegal', even though they had to enter the country through unconventional methods? Should I point out that they must be in a dire situation to risk their lives trying to stow themselves away under lorries or on precarious boats, though many die in the process? Should I articulate how unfair it seems that some of us can enjoy easy travel for leisure while others are expected to remain in contexts of conflict and poverty because they lack the resources and freedom of movement afforded to a privileged few?

Before I could decide what to say, or even whether or not it was appropriate to challenge what had merely been a throwaway comment, the conversation had moved on to the holiday in Paris that had preceded this glimpse of asylum seekers from the comfort of a Eurostar train.

It wasn't the first time I'd heard such comments and I knew it wouldn't be the last.

Thinking about our attitudes towards asylum seekers

My friend's remarks weren't meant to offend me or anyone in particular. They were simply a genuine and personal reaction to a situation that had confronted her. They made me sad, however, because – as someone who has worked with refugees and asylum seekers for many years – I had hoped that Christians at least could be more empathetic towards the plight of others, especially those desperately seeking safety.

But as Christians we are not immune to the negative mess of emotions which the presence, or potential presence, of displaced people from elsewhere can engender, such as fear, self preservation, guilt, denial and confusion. Fear that our country is overcrowded and that our finite resources won't stretch to others. Guilt that we have so much by global standards yet feel so powerless in the face of overwhelming economic and material need. A desire to simply look the other way, justifying our own lack of engagement by readily accepting a language which erroneously dismisses these anonymous newcomers as 'bogus'. Even as someone who ought to know better, I admit to feeling real anxiety when reading an article by someone in an affluent part of the country exhorting us all to share our spare rooms with refugees. Working in the voluntary sector in London, I can barely afford a room of my own, let alone a spare one.

However, especially when the Syrian refugee crisis of 2015 brought the reality of forced displacement closer to home, even to countries usually buffered by distance and borders, the Church reacted with love and hope. Indeed, many Christians were, and have been since, at the forefront of the 'refugee crisis' response. They have met practical needs by offering money, time, clothing and accommodation. They have matched this compassion by calling for justice and speaking out about the policy and practice which affect both the people who have fled conflict and persecution and the situations which have caused their flight in the first place.

Some people seeking refuge also turn up in our churches; in the same way that everyone else comes to church for a whole range of reasons, so asylum seekers come with a variety of motivations. Some come because they are attracted by the love of Christians or because they already follow Christ, some seek safety after coming to faith if they fear return to their country of origin, and others may want help to strengthen their application to remain in the UK.

This chapter seeks to address some of the questions that churches have raised when individual asylum seekers become part of their congregations, particularly those from Muslim backgrounds who have either come to faith during their time in the UK or are seeking safety from religious persecution in Muslim-majority countries. How should churches respond with love and wisdom to those going through a complicated and daunting asylum system?

Cultivating a biblical view of asylum seekers

It is always great to see Christians taking action in response to the situation of asylum seekers, but why should it come as a surprise to see the Church rising up in response to this particular manifestation of suffering and injustice? For surely the church should be full of people who see the inherent value of others created in the image of God, of those who have experienced grace and generosity in their own lostness and poverty? Are we not people who can freely spend ourselves on behalf of others, through confidence in a God who replenishes our resources, meets our needs, and tells us not to be afraid; a God from whom everything comes in the first place?

As Christians, we follow Jesus who himself had been a refugee with his parents when they fled a despotic and murderous tyrant. As Jesus' fearful parents escaped their home country and sought safety elsewhere, he would have been about the same age as Syrian toddler Alan Kurdi, the image of whose small lifeless body washed up on a beach prompted a massive outpouring of compassion and calls for justice even among those who had previously been immune to the unfolding 'refugee crisis'.

The church is called to follow the itinerant Jesus, building on a longer biblical tradition of migration, from the time that Abraham was called to leave a settled place for the land that God was promising him, to the Exodus and the Exile. We are frequently reminded that as citizens of his Kingdom we are also aliens and strangers here, journeying towards a heavenly city that God has prepared for us.

Woven throughout the Bible's narrative of journey, we also see the foreigner not as a threat or object of pity but as a blessing and example. Melchizedek blessed God's people,[1] the Queen of Sheba brought her wealth to Solomon[2], while Ruth the Moabite committed to her mother-in-law's God and nation and became the great-grandmother of David.[3] In the New Testament it was a Samaritan who became the archetypal model of a good neighbour[4], a Roman centurion who showed unparalleled faith[5], and a Syro-Phoencian woman whose understanding of Jesus' mission was greater than that of many of his own disciples[6].

It is hard to read the Bible without hearing its constant counter-cultural approach towards the stranger or seeing migration and displacement as central to the biblical narrative and our own Christian identity.

Who are asylum seekers anyway?

So what, in technical terms and our context, is a refugee? The word is used by different people in different ways but in terms of international law has a particular

---

1   Genesis 14: 18-20, NIV.
2   1 Kings 10: 1-13, NIV.
3   Ruth 1: 16-18, Ruth 4: 16-22, NIV.
4   Luke 10:25-37, NIV.
5   Luke 7:1-10, NIV.
6   Mark 7:24-30, NIV.

definition, set out in the 1951 Refugee Convention, a treaty originally created to respond to mass displacement in Europe after the Second World War. In the Refugee Convention, which also sets out the rights of individuals granted asylum and the responsibilities of the nations which bestow it, a refugee is defined as a person who,

> owing to a well-founded fear of being persecuted for reasons of race, religion, nationality, membership of a particular social group or political opinion, is outside the country of his nationality, and is unable to, or owing to such fear, is unwilling to avail himself of the protection of that country.[7]

An asylum seeker is someone who is asking to be recognised as a refugee. They believe that they would be at risk of persecution in the country they have come from and are seeking protection elsewhere. Although this administrative term has become laden with negative connotations, there is nothing inherently illegal or fraudulent about the people it describes.

In fact, the label 'asylum seeker' is very often the only thing that asylum seekers have in common. An asylum seeker might be a doctor from Syria from an affluent family background, or an orphaned teenager from Afghanistan who has never had any formal education. An asylum seeker might be a mechanic from Iraq, an artist from Eritrea, a teacher from Pakistan, or an engineer from Sudan. They might be young or old, male or female, Christian or Muslim, married or single, from a rich or poor background. When we hear someone described as an asylum seeker, all we really know about them is that they are a person who is seeking safety in a country which is not their own.

How does the asylum process work?

In reality, most people fleeing persecution end up in countries closer to where they are from. At the end of 2015, over four million Syrian refugees were in Turkey, Lebanon, Jordan and Iraq, a vast figure compared to the several hundred thousand seeking safety in Europe. Likewise, around 95% of the 2.6 million Afghans displaced by war and insecurity reside in Iran and Pakistan, compared to less than 2,000 who claimed asylum in the UK in 2014.

When people are resettled, such as the estimated 20,000 Syrians who are anticipated to be given a home in the UK in the coming years, they do not need to claim asylum on arrival. However, any others arriving in search of safety must go through an official process, designed to identify who fits the specific criteria of a 'refugee' under the Refugee Convention. People are generally expected to claim asylum as soon as they arrive in a 'safe' country. Once someone has claimed asylum, officials look into evidence of their case, seeking to identify if their fear

---

7   www.unhcr.org/pages/49c3646c125.html

of persecution on the specified grounds is, indeed, 'well-founded'.

This section focuses particularly on the UK asylum process in which people have a brief initial screening interview where they are asked on what grounds they fear persecution. People's responses must be as accurate and detailed as possible because any contradictions in the later more substantive interview will stand against them.

Although all this makes intuitive sense to all those who want to ensure a correct process for assessing 'genuine refugees', it is worth remembering why discrepancies in people's accounts may arise. Consider, for example, the situation of a woman who had been raped in a country where those in government institutions are to be feared not trusted. Is it surprising that she may not disclose intimate details straightaway in an interview with unknown officials? Or the predicament of an Afghan 15 year old, asked detailed questions about life in his homeland shortly after arriving in the UK after a year's journey by foot, boat and lorry, who may then remember additional information after a period of convalescence and support. Along similar lines, converts may, through fear of disclosing their conversion to a Muslim official or for other reasons, demonstrate an inconsistency between interviews which may subsequently damage their 'credibility'.

The initial screening interview is followed at some point by a fuller interview. Many people are 'refused' (not granted asylum) at this stage. Cases of conversion have been refused on the grounds that the conversion is not genuine and that the convert could escape detection and/or persecution if they were sent back to their own country, although recent cases have suggested that a 'duty to evangelise' makes this unreasonable.

Cases like this go to an appeals stage. In an asylum tribunal, barristers for the Home Office and the asylum seeker argue their cases (though many asylum seekers are unable to secure the support of a barrister and must argue their cases themselves); drawing on evidence and statements prepared by solicitors, an independent judge makes a decision.

If the judge accepts that the asylum seeker's case is well-founded, they grant them protection in the UK, sometimes in the form of 'refugee status' and sometimes 'humanitarian protection'. Both come with 5 years leave to remain in the UK and bestow a range of entitlements which enable people to work, travel, study, and move forward with their lives. After 5 years, people can apply for an extension of their leave to remain.

If the judge rejects the case, a person still has further opportunities to appeal, though the chance of winning at these stages appears to decrease. Those who are refused at every stage eventually become 'appeal rights exhausted' (ARE). Although people still have the opportunity to put in a fresh claim for asylum, this requires new evidence and changes in circumstances. At this stage, most people are expected to make arrangements to return to their country. Some are required to report regularly at the Home Office during this time, and some are detained in immigration removal centres (commonly called detention centres). If a person does not return, they face forced removal. Some people are unable to return so remain in the UK, destitute and unsupported.

While the aim of the asylum process is to identify those in need of protection, many argue that the system is flawed and that so much depends on factors like the competence and commitment of individual solicitors, the accuracy of translation processes, and the attitude of particular judges. The amount of asylum refusals overturned at the appeal stage, and the number of people who later go on to receive refugee status even after periods of being Appeal Rights Exhausted, are just a few of the grounds on which to question the quality and fairness of the current system and challenge the dehumanising effect it has on those going through it.

Although asylum systems vary in different countries, taking different lengths of time and affording asylum seekers different levels of care and support, going through the UK's asylum process is, for many, an exhausting and damaging experience.

What is life like for an asylum seeker?

It's not easy being an asylum seeker.

Asylum seekers are grieving the absence of family and friends and face the challenge of coping with a new culture and a new language. The long periods of uncertain waiting while their cases are being scrutinised can have detrimental psychological impacts on those going through the asylum process.

Bearing in mind that people have already undergone traumatic and difficult changes, whether by escaping persecution in their home country or leaving their cultural community through conversion, the uncertainty about the outcome of their asylum claim and the complexity of the process makes life extremely difficult. There are often huge variations in the length of time people have to wait and in the requirements imposed on people (for example some people have to report regularly at the Home Office or are detained, while others face no restrictions), and many feel that there are discrepancies in the outcomes of apparently similar cases. The system often appears arbitrary and opaque for those going through it and can make people angry, depressed, and confused.

The very term 'asylum seeker', technically an administrative category, can have damaging implications on the people it labels. Negative press and a lack of understanding has changed it into a dehumanising term, laden with associations of illegality and a lack of credibility. Ali, a teenager from Iraq, told me that he had never let any of his school friends know that he was an asylum seeker. He was so worried about how he would be perceived that he covered it up, avoiding social events which would be too expensive for him, telling his classmates he was busy when he had to go to a meeting with his solicitor, and avoiding becoming too close to friends in case they found out he was an asylum seeker and rejected him. His desire to be a 'normal teenager' was overwhelming and keeping up the façade was exhausting.

Sara, another person seeking asylum reiterated this by saying:

> I am sick of not having an identity. As an asylum seeker here you have no identity, you are always waiting. I want to be recognised as belonging, to be able to make my contribution.

Being an asylum seeker also has very practical implications. In the UK context, asylum seekers are not allowed to work and must rely on a weekly payment of just £36.95 (at the time of writing), which is about half the allowance given to job seekers in the UK. Although asylum seekers are sometimes branded 'benefit scroungers', the reality is that they have no right to claim any welfare benefits, and many have never even come across the concept before; most would much prefer to use their time and skills to work, support themselves, and make a contribution to society. In some cases, asylum seeker payments come in the form of vouchers which can only be used in particular supermarkets, not in cheaper shops or markets which sell the type of food they may prefer to eat and where their money could go further. These financial constraints make it hard for people to live 'normal' life, unable to afford bus or train fares, top up phone credit, have meals out, and do other things that commonly help develop friendships and build community. Their access to housing, healthcare and education is very limited and it is not uncommon for asylum seekers to end up in real destitution.

Because asylum seekers are all unique individuals, united simply by their legal status as people waiting for decisions on their protection claims, these psychological and practical challenges affect different people in different ways.

Try to imagine what it would be like for you.

Imagine if you had left your home country under stressful circumstances and were grieving the loss of your family and culture. Imagine if every aspect of your life and faith came under scrutiny and your character was grilled to see if you were 'credible'. Imagine if you were not allowed to work and if all your skills and experience were devalued and you couldn't provide for yourself or your family. Imagine if you were not able to offer hospitality to others and had to always be the recipient of charity. Imagine if you had to cope with a complex system and do everything in a second language, unable to communicate your unique personality, ideas and hopes to those around you. Imagine if you were unable to engage in political processes or to progress in education. Imagine if you had to try to live from one day to the next, never quite knowing if the system would work out in your favour or where you were going to end up.

What role can churches play?

Although I had got to know many asylum seekers through my job in a local charity, and grappled long and hard with the practical and justice issues that the situation of refugees raised, for me it was Maryam who first brought all these things into my church context.

Maryam was a warm, intelligent, Muslim woman who had moved from the Middle East to pursue postgraduate studies in a British university, her fees and living expenses funded by her government. Missing her husband and the familiarity of home, she readily accepted invitations from a friend of mine to meals and then to church. Though speaking very little English, she nevertheless threw herself into these new communities, keen to make friends and to express herself to people who made time to listen.

Her conversion changed everything. Fearful of the implications of her newfound faith if she were to return home, she claimed asylum in the UK. In doing so, she lost so much. She lost contact with family and friends she cared about and access to her financial resources and the status she had once enjoyed at home. She lost the funding for her education and living expenses, and she faced court hearings where she was grilled about this new faith she had encountered.

As she emerged shivering and spluttering but utterly joyful from the river where she was baptised, I saw properly for the first time the real implications of the choice that she had made. For Maryam, it would not be enough to encourage her along to a midweek 'home group', where she would sit for an hour and a half over tea and biscuits to speak about the struggles of having 'quiet times' and praying for courage to overcome British embarrassment about inviting colleagues to a church event. The challenges she'd face would be much more severe than that.

"Help!" I knew that some of us were thinking, "There's an asylum seeker in our church!"

In Maryam's situation, and in the situations of others I subsequently got to know, the churches involved rose to the challenge of this new adventure of working out how to love and be family to the asylum-seeking sisters and brothers with which God had blessed them.

Practical support

> Whether you become a follower of Jesus or not... we will love you for who you are, we will love you anyway, and we will try and help you to get a better quality of life.[8]

Love towards those in our churches seeking asylum outworks itself in practical ways. At the most basic level, this involves responding to those practical needs brought about by people's status both as asylum seekers and as culturally-displaced people who are adjusting to life in a new context.

---

8   Church leader speaking to an asylum-seeking member of his congregation.

A family in 23 year old Zahra's church invited her to stay in the room of their son who had just left for university. She had been ready to start university in her own country and longed to start training as a dentist, but this all now seemed like an unrealistic dream. Realising that access to education was a complex process, but that it meant so much to her, members of Zahra's church introduced her to a charity which gave her accurate advice about ways of continuing to study. This re-inspired her and she started going along to her church's friendship café for international students where she could spend time with fun and thoughtful people who liked to talk about interesting things. One week, one of the volunteers told her that it wasn't really the best place for her as her situation was different and she wasn't actually a student. Zahra got upset, felt singled out and stopped going.

She missed her mother and sister and wondered if she would ever be able to see them again, and she constantly felt the weight of her asylum case hanging over her. People from the church often had Zahra round for dinner and picked her up for a midweek group so she didn't have to pay for the bus but could have the opportunity to grow in her faith with others. Someone helped her find a place where she could volunteer in the day to give her a sense of structure and purpose, and others took her away for a weekend to enjoy a rare change of scene.

It wasn't always easy for Zahra or for the wider church. There was always a balance to be struck of recognising her practical needs as an asylum seeker, while not wanting to single her out or define her by her immigration status. The church had to think creatively about what it meant to Zahra as a gifted member of the church family, able to serve and give in spite of everything she lacked, to be respected not just pitied, and to be enabled to contribute instead of always being the recipient of aid. It couldn't just depend on one or two people making an effort, but was a community effort and a reciprocal one.

I thought of Zahra the other day as I sat in my old bedroom at my parents' house having moved back in for a few months. I missed having a home where I could invite my friends round and wished I could access all my personal things that were in storage. I felt despondent about my limited housing options and the possibility for change. I was so grateful for my parents' generosity in having me there, knowing that it came at a cost to them, but sometimes felt stuck and frustrated. As I moaned to myself, I remembered what Zahra had said to me:

> They are all so generous and kind and they are lovely people. Sometimes I just want to scream but I don't want to be ungrateful. If I didn't have them, I don't know what I would do, but I can't really choose anything that I am doing at the moment.

Although her situation was so much worse than mine, I got an insight into how it really felt. And I was inspired again by the way that she had been so gracious in all the times she felt disempowered, grateful rather than critical, and able to recognise the love which underpinned people's actions.

As with any family, being part of a church requires grace, love and perseverance on both sides, and the same is just as true for brothers and sisters in the asylum process as it is for the rest of us.

Support with people's asylum cases

However, as churches we can't ignore the fact that the asylum seeker label carries very unique restrictions and political implications, and that loving asylum seekers requires us to engage in this complex reality and to pursue justice in a flawed context.

It is worth remembering that the asylum process is a legal one and it is vital that asylum seekers have a good solicitor to represent them. If a person is claiming asylum on grounds of religious persecution or conversion, they don't necessarily need a Christian solicitor. However, they do need someone who sensitively understands the issues around conversion and who can help a person build a strong case through expert evidence and supportive witness statements. In spite of recent cuts to legal aid funding for immigration cases, asylum cases are covered by legal aid. However, it can often be challenging to find a good local legal aid solicitor who is able to take on a case straightaway, and it is tempting for people to turn to more unscrupulous legal representatives. A church can help their asylum-seeking brothers and sisters to find a registered and reputable solicitor, perhaps drawing on personal recommendations and networks. Even if they are unsure where to start, churches can signpost people to expert refugee organisations to assist in this process.

There are many other ways that churches can support asylum seekers through this legal process. Abbas' friends, for example, helped him to read and understand the letters he received from the Home Office and his solicitor. When he needed to make phone calls, they let him use their landline phones so he did not have to spend all his phone credit while on hold, and sometimes they made phone calls on his behalf to advocate for all the support and clarification he needed, especially when he was fearful that asking for more information and support may in some way be detrimental to his case. They went with him to his daunting asylum tribunal and to meetings with his solicitor. They knew it would have taken a long time and most of his weekly income to reach these appointments on public transport, especially as most required travelling at peak times to make it to appointments first thing in the morning. At one stage, when he was required to report at the Home Office, they made sure they knew when he was going and called him afterwards to see if he was OK. Their support helped him feel less alone in a complex process.

When someone is claiming asylum on the basis of conversion, the church leader is often regarded as an expert witness to the 'veracity' of the person's faith. The church leader's statement and presence at a tribunal does carry weight. Bearing witness to a person's faith requires reference to their attendance at worship, their involvement in other features of church life, their knowledge of aspects of the Bible, and a statement that their baptism is not one of convenience, as this will often be the suspicion of the Home Office. The statement should be signed and dated, written on headed paper and is strengthened by the church leader giving evidence in person at the hearing.

It is important not to assume any knowledge in the Home Office about Christianity (in a recent hearing, the barrister for the Home Office challenged someone by saying "but according to Google...") and to recognise that they may make unreasonable and arbitrary assumptions of Christians, such as a 'true' Christian would be able to recite the books of the Bible and name all the disciples. The church leader's statement could, for example, explain the church's mode of worship so that Home Office officials not to use their own preconceptions to misjudge the asylum seeker (for example, specify the modes of worship so they are not asked questions about liturgy which may be unfamiliar) and should avoid phrases (such as 'knows Jesus Christ') which may not have any meaning outside a church context. Churches can help people prepare for their tribunals in a way that enables them to confidently speak the truth in a daunting and interrogative context.

When church leaders and members testify to an asylum seeker's faith, they are doing just that. They are not expected to be experts who know all about a person's country of origin and the risks they'd face on return, but they should simply testify to the faith and their experience of a person. The solicitor will help compile other information about a person's country of origin to counter the likely arguments that a believer could safely relocate within their country of origin or practice their faith discreetly. However, there is a role for churches in signposting solicitors to sources of information which may be unfamiliar to them, such as Christian NGOs (like Christian Solidarity Worldwide, Open Doors and World Watch Monitor) who could supply evidence about religious persecution in particular counties and regions (while recognising, however, that such generic information is not in itself enough as the asylum process is seeking to determine the specific threat against an individual). The Asylum Advocacy Group may also be able to assist.

Whatever the outcome

When someone ceases to be an asylum seeker because their immigration status changes, for better or worse, they do not cease to being a part of the church community. Even when a person is granted refugee status, a positive outcome, they nevertheless enter yet another time of transition and begin the next stage of their journey. Their need for love and support continues.

The reality is that some people, who we have got to know and come to love, may be refused asylum and face the prospect of return to their own countries. At this stage, as throughout the entire process, churches can seek to disciple people in a worldview that everything is under God's control, even when everything feels uncertain and threatening. This can be a terrifying time and some people decide to risk a precarious life in the UK under the radar of the authorities rather than go back to a place where they still fear persecution. Others return, either voluntarily or through force, and churches can do what they can to prepare them for this reality, including by putting them in touch with believers in the countries to which they are returning. It is worth contacting persecuted church agencies, such as Release International, or para-church networks such as Middle East Concern, for assistance in brokering these relationships.

Before being removed, and even at other stages in the asylum process, some people are put into detention centres. Although these centres have chaplaincies and various forms of religious support, some Muslim converts may be fearful of engaging with these due to threats from those who oppose their alignment to Christianity, and it is critical that churches continue to support and visit those who could, at this stage, easily be as out of mind as they are of sight.

The first time I went into a detention centre I was very much out of my comfort zone. Even though I had my British passport as ID, I still felt a bit violated as I was thoroughly searched on my way in, and had to grapple with my anger that people could be locked up for having had the misfortune of being born in the wrong part of the world. As I walked into the dreary room, where tables crudely separated detainees from their visitors and where tokenistic posters about humanity and respect jarred with the prison-like context, I wondered what on earth I would say to Sajid who was facing forced return to a volatile context. How could I possibly offer any kind of hope? We sat opposite each other, sometimes in silence and sometimes laughing at past memories or speaking honestly about fears, and I realised that there was something sacred about simply being there. Empty-handed and deeply inadequate, I nevertheless knew that God was tangibly present, even in a place where the light doesn't seem to shine.

Prayer

It's not just in detention centres that everything can appear completely out of our control. Whether we are offering practical support, speaking out about injustice, or working out how to love and be loved by those from very different cultural backgrounds, the power of prayer cannot be downplayed.

Abdul is an asylum seeker who I got to know well. The precarious nature of his situation was affecting every part of his life and having a detrimental impact on his physical and mental health. He wanted me to help him but I simply didn't know what to do, and I don't think he did either. I felt powerless to change anything and, before I really knew what I was doing, heard myself asking if he wanted me to pray with him. Even as I said it I felt a bit silly. Who was I to pray for someone who was so stuck? What did I expect God to do? Fix everything? Pull him out of depression? Grant him leave to remain in the UK?

Nevertheless, he said yes, so I prayed for him. I found myself simply praying that he would know that he was loved and valued by a God who knew him inside out, who was with him in the darkness and who offered hope. In some ways it felt so insufficient and he left with the same complex difficulties with which he'd arrived. He came back to see me the following week because he wanted to tell me something. He said:

> I just wanted to tell you that things are different. I mean, nothing has really changed, but it feels like something has changed. I've been trying to work it out because everything is the same, but I feel different and have more peace. I wanted to tell you this because the only different thing last week was when you prayed for me.

It encouraged me that God's activity is not bound by immigration status and that any of us, in spite of our lack of power and understanding, can pray.

How can you tell if someone is a 'real' Christian?

> He told us that he needed a letter to support his asylum case because he wouldn't be safe if he went back to his country. He wants people from the church to back up the fact that he's a Christian. We know that he's been coming along to church for a while but it's hard to know where he's really 'at', if you know what I mean.[9]

When someone's asylum claim rests on fear of religious persecution, for example if they would face persecution as a Christian in their country of origin or because they have come to faith since their arrival in the UK, the 'genuineness' of their faith comes under scrutiny, not only by the Home Office but by members of the churches of which they are a part.

But how do you prove if someone's faith is 'genuine'? Is it about being baptised? Or having an in depth knowledge of the Bible? Or going to church regularly and being part of a small group? Or demonstrating tangible signs of the Holy Spirit at work? And how do you prove this anyway?

During a recent period of depression, I have rarely been to church. I haven't had the energy to see my Christian friends or go to midweek groups and talk about anything deep and meaningful. I have struggled to read the Bible and have felt distant from God. Had my right to remain in the UK hung on a requirement to prove my Christian identity in the way that an asylum seeker would need to, I think I would have been removed from the country months ago. Fortunately my British passport has given me the freedom and security to work things through at my own pace with the support I've needed. Asylum seekers claiming protection on religious grounds do not enjoy this privilege.

---

9   Members of a church congregation speaking about an asylum-seeking person in their church.

There is no easy answer to these questions. Pastor Ian Jones talked about the signs of conversion he looked for:

> You see the development of them, the change in their countenance and the way that they use terms like "I don't feel like I'm an orphan anymore", so you hear them speaking terms that they wouldn't understand. You discern there's spiritual revelation that only can come through the Holy Spirit. So there's that aspect that you look for.
>
> Then there's the fruit in their lives, when they say, "I used to be so nasty to people, I was judgmental, but now I find I'm loving people, now I'm forgiving people". So it's not just the words of the mouth, it's the content of the heart that begins to be exposed, and then you think, "I can see fruit, not just confession, but fruit of conversion here".
>
> And then obviously they are ready when they say, "I want to get baptised". Before we baptise them, I will want to sit with them with Javed, (a church member who speaks their own language) to ask them questions so that they can express in their own language exactly what's going on in their heart, their understanding of the person of Jesus, why he died, where he is now, and the love of the Father and things like that. You can't fake that stuff. When we are both sure, and others are sure, then we baptise them.[10]

However, not all cases appear so clear cut. As discussed elsewhere in this book, many believers from Muslim backgrounds face threats from those who oppose their conversion, which in turn impacts their ability to openly articulate and practice, let alone share, their faith. Others may come to faith having claimed asylum on different grounds (such as political persecution) and may not realise that their conversion could have any impact on their case. Not every asylum seeker necessarily understands the value of supporting statements nor requests them, and some may even feel fearful about speaking out about their conversion, even if it could strengthen their application. Some may simply be on a spiritual journey and, although their changing worldview could put them at increased risk on return, may not be ready to make a commitment or to get baptised, even though ticking this box could have positive impacts on their claim for protection.

And there are times that we may feel like we've got it 'wrong'. Ali and Saffiyah had been warmly welcomed into the church. They threw themselves into the life of that community and there was much celebration at the way they were growing in their faith. People went with them to their asylum hearings, wrote supporting statements, spent time getting to know them and were generous in their care towards them. But soon as they were granted refugee status they disappeared.

---

10 *Joining the Family* course.

They stopped coming to church and they didn't respond to people's efforts to contact them. People in the church felt hurt, used and disappointed, and many never wanted to engage with asylum seekers again.

But perhaps it's not all that different to the families who start coming to church or get their children christened as they prepare to apply for a good local school. It's possible that they are doing so strategically to strengthen their children's school applications but it is also possible that they simply want community and are exploring faith for themselves. In the same way that we accept them at face value and take opportunities to articulate and demonstrate the gospel, so we love and journey with asylum seekers in our churches. It is genuinely painful to feel duped or used. and I wonder how Jesus felt investing in those who would go on to betray or deny him. Love for others always makes us vulnerable, yet love is what we are called to nonetheless.

A vicar friend of mine did all that he could to support Bilal, a recent convert from Islam in his church community who wanted to be baptised. They read the Bible together for many months and my friend supported him as much as he could through the asylum process. However, Bilal was eventually refused and put into a detention centre while awaiting his removal in the UK. My friend visited him regularly, sometimes speaking about how he could continue to be a Christian on his return to South Asia and sometimes just being a friend in a lonely and scary place. I knew that he'd often doubted Bilal's underlying motivations in church involvement so I asked him why he'd bothered to carry on seeing him once he was detained. My friend answered simply:

> My role as his minister is to care for him and disciple him. It's not my place to judge or to be an immigration officer. He's part of my church family whether he is in detention or not.

Part of the family

My friend's words are a good reminder that asylum seekers in our churches are first and foremost individual human beings, and need to be treated as such. Sometimes this seems to be forgotten when a person is going through a complex and daunting asylum process which has such significant practical, psychological and legal implications on all aspects of their life.

Nevertheless, in the same way that we respond to needs among other members of the church family, such as by cooking meals for parents of a new baby or inviting an international student over for lunch, so can we respond in practical ways to those going through this asylum process by, for example, offering direct assistance where their resources are limited, ensuring they have the support they need to access more specialist advice, care and information, advocating for justice when their voices are ignored, engaging in the political processes which affect them, and ensuring that truth and generosity prevail in our words and actions.

Imagining ourselves in asylum-seeking shoes is perhaps a good starting point for treating people the way we would hope to be treated were our roles reversed.

As we experience the messy complexity and beautiful richness of a church which both spans national borders and is locally situated, our twofold challenge is to remember that God's plans to give his people a hope and a future are not limited by immigration status and to work out how to live in the light of that reality.

POINTS TO PONDER:

1 What emotions do you feel when you hear the words 'asylum seeker'?

2 How could your church help people seeking asylum while also showing them respect?

3 What particular guidelines does this chapter give for how to support asylum seekers who are Christ's followers of Muslim background?

Joining the Family

CHAPTER TWELVE

The long journey home

(Roxy writing…)

> The church is that single, multiethnic family promised by the creator God to Abraham. It was brought into being through Israel's Messiah, Jesus; it was energized by God's Spirit; and it was called to bring the transformative news of God's rescuing Justice to the whole creation.[1]

We are all on a journey home to the Father. We have talked about birth identity and the new identity but the journey to becoming more like Jesus doesn't finish at conversion; it continues through life. For many believers from Muslim backgrounds the journey may be quite traumatic to begin with, and then it settles into a rhythm as they learn more about what their new life looks like as a follower of Jesus. On this journey long term adjustment is needed and this affects every part of the individual's life.

Identity and culture

You can't talk about identity without talking about culture, as who you are is tangled up with culture and religion. That's one of the reasons why identity is so complex for believers of Muslim background because even after being a believer for a long time you keep coming back to this shift between cultures and religions. Events in life remind you and make you feel like you've still got a way to go on the journey of belonging. Significant times in your life, like getting married or having your first child, remind you of where you've come from and the new identity you have in Christ. Questions such as "Who am I?", "Where do I belong?", and "What is my culture?" keep coming back.

---

1   N T Wright, *Simply Christian*, (SPCK Publishing, 2011), p.200.

It seems that some BMBs, in rejecting Islam and their culture, find their identity in that rejection and take a very polemical approach. There are also BMBs who feel a closeness to their birth culture and family, and consequently are less angry with Islam. Thus Khalad Hussein writes in his book *Against the Grain*:

Khalad

Lord, thank you! Thank you for my birthplace and heritage. Thank you for my parents and the foundations they were able to lay for my life.[2]

Similarly, Nabeel Qureshi speaks so lovingly of his parents when he dedicates his book to them:

Nabeel

Ammi and Abba, your undying love for me even when I have sinned against you is only second to God's love for his children.[3]

Sometimes a new believer at first adopts everything about the new identity enthusiastically including the community and culture, and rejects everything about the old. But over the years he or she comes to critique aspects of the new, and to appreciate aspects of the old. *Spiritually* the person has gone from death to life, has a new birth, goes from darkness to light et cetera, but *culturally* and *relationally* and *psychologically* it's not that simple. "The old is never fully erased; the new is overwritten on the old" says Rudolf Heredia, author and academic.[4] And no one human culture is ever a perfect reflection of God's ways anyway.

Those who have gone through a radical change from old to new identity may hanker after the old, many years later. They are not rejecting their faith in Christ, but they are renegotiating their identity in relation to community and culture. This may take a long time. Even after twenty years of being a believer there are certain things about being a Muslim in a Muslim community that I miss and hanker after. For instance, the 'Iftar' meal at the end of a day of fasting during Ramadan, used to be a really special family time and we used to have the most delicious food during that time.

Or sometimes, when the Christian path gets lonely or laborious, a BMB longs to go back to what's familiar, what's comfortable, what they imbibed as a child, like a set of comfortable old clothes that fit without having to struggle. I think of two friends who talked about 'going back to Islam' but I don't think they were saying Islam is better, or that they were intellectually convinced of it. No, what they meant was "the Muslim way of life is easier because it's familiar, it's comfortable, and I would have my family around me".

---

2   Khalad Hussein, Against The Grain, (Xlibris Publishing, 2012), p.189.
3   Nabeel Qureshi, Seeking Allah, Finding Jesus, (Zondervan, 2014), Dedication.
4   Rudolf Heredia, Changing Gods: Rethinking Conversion in India. (Penguin, 2007), p.127.

For the Christian mentor it can feel quite shocking when your BMB friend says they want to go back to Islam, when you thought they were doing so well in their discipleship, so why the doubts now? But we need to see past the presenting issue to the underlying one. "I want to go back to Islam" might just be a cry for help and comfort; it might be a BMB's way of expressing their loneliness and their longing for community and family.

In our western context, even when we talk about the family of God and all of us being part of that family we sometimes feel threatened by the idea of family. For believers from Muslim backgrounds the threat is more about not belonging – about being on their own, being without family. Over the long term they will seek to settle in a church community and family.

As they seek family and a place to belong, they may choose to be part of a British church and a BMB fellowship where they feel a sense of belonging. There are BMBs all over the UK who go to an Iranian Fellowship during the week but also attend (and many are members of) a British church. BMB fellowships can serve a variety of roles. They can be a bridge for outreach, or a get-together with likeminded people who know where they are coming from, or a growing place for discipleship and ministry, or all of the above. They can also be a place to affirm a 'third space' identity where BMBs as a group can say "we're not Muslim, we're not white British middle-class Christian, but we are a group together as Christ's followers of Muslim background and this is an expression of our identity". People can belong to such a group as well as belonging to a British church. This is a choice that each person makes for themselves.

Life continues after conversion

> *Jesus replied; "Anyone who loves me will obey my teaching. My Father will love them and we will come to them and make our home with them".* [5]

After believers have made the decision to follow Jesus and become his disciple, life continues and they need to continue to learn and grow, as all believers do. This growth happens throughout life - in times of celebration, doubt and trouble. Growth ebbs and flows, as life is often like a rollercoaster with Jesus. We find that when difficult things happen we may need to cling to God; we have a growth spurt as a result of that intimacy with God. At other times it may be that we feel God is distant because we don't have that sense of his presence in our lives. But Jesus says, "My Father will love them and we will come to them and make our home with them", so whatever happens God promises to be with us. For BMBs this distance can seem extremely difficult after the initial conversion and baptism highs. It may mean they seem to go into a time of being quite low

---

5   John 14:23, NIV.

and feeling lonely. Sometimes churches leave them to deal with this lonely and difficult time all on their own but this is when they need their mentor, small group and wider church to support and encourage them with words, actions and understanding, enabling them to keep their eyes on Jesus and reminding them of those that have gone before them.

Ongoing relationship with a mentor

As a believer grows up in his or her faith the needs change and therefore the relationship with the mentor needs to change. It may mean that the relationship becomes more like that of friends together and that you spend less time studying and more time enjoying each other's company, socialising and praying together. It may mean the BMB decides he doesn't need to have an ongoing mentor as he needs time to live out his faith and test what he has learnt. They may be more able to find the support and encouragement they need in small groups and in church friendships. They may also be mature enough to find answers to their questions in the Bible and in prayer times with God. This is all important for the continuous growth of a believer.

It may be difficult for a mentor to let go at this time just as when children leave home for the first time; it feels like a big change and can leave you feeling bereft. But it is important to let go in order for the person to be free to walk the path God has for them. The relationship will inevitably continue to be special and you may still see each other often but it will be more as friends or brothers and sisters in Christ. It's so important that you have been walking with them up until now, and they may still come to you and ask for wisdom and advice as they continue on their journey. Don't underestimate how important it has been for them to have you walk with them and the sacrifices you have made will bear much fruit in their lives. You may not see the fruit immediately but over the years it will become more and more evident.

I didn't realise how important the first years of meeting with an individual mentor were for me until much later. I realised that they had helped me to lay the foundations of my faith deep into the God of love. They had studied the Bible with me every week; they had taught me much about daily prayer and conversation with God. They had taught me to put what I learnt from the Bible into practice and to trust God in difficult times. For example I learnt that deciding to sing and worship God even when I find it difficult to believe he is with me, is sometimes an act of obedience that God honours and delights in, and through it I have received healing and peace in my soul.

Enabling BMBs to make a life for themselves

Settling into life as a believer may take a long time for some people, as life can be complicated and difficulties can hinder their sense of belonging in the Muslim and/

or Christian community. Part of this settling into life as a believer may involve getting married and having children as you join a new family, as Tim Green describes:

Tim

One aspect of long-term identity is marriage, because that gives you a new family to belong to (your in-laws) and can lead on to starting your own new branch in the family line. One BMB told me how pleased he was when his daughter was born, to think "This is the first Christian child born in generations of my family". Also, who you marry has a big impact on whether your spiritual identity has the chance to flourish or not. Or if you don't get married that may get increasingly difficult for single BMBs as they get into middle age or beyond. [6]

Many of us find belonging and identity from forming our own new physical family when we find a husband or wife. I know that the gift of marriage for me was also a gift of a new home, a place to truly be myself and belong. The following verse in Psalm 84 has meant a lot to me and really represents what God wants for all of us to experience as we make our home with him.

Even the sparrow has found a home and the swallow a nest for herself where she may have her young.[7]

Marriage can give us a place of long term security in addition to having the church as family. As that is likely to include parents in law and grandparents and brothers and sisters, the believer's family has immediately got bigger. I have found that especially as our marriage is cross-cultural, both my husband and I have needed to learn to communicate well about our behavior and expectations. We've needed to realise when change needs to happen and when a cultural thing is helpful to us and our relationship. For example, I have always loved curry and therefore I often cook Pakistani curry and my husband has enjoyed that!!! But I also sometimes behave in a way just to avoid shame, and I don't need to do that anymore. Cross cultural marriages are enriched by two cultures coming together but they can also be complicated by the expectations of both parties of what marriage is and the roles of men and women in marriage and more. (The book *Love Across Latitudes*[8] explores this in more detail). The excitement of new ways of seeing life and the world together, and the challenges of learning new behaviours and stepping into another person's world, go hand in hand in cross cultural marriages. Like anyone else, BMBs may need support as they prepare for marriage - going through a marriage course and learning about God's heart for the relationship between husband and wife might be a start. This applies whether the

---

6   Personal conversation.
7   Psalm 84:3, NIV.
8   Janet Fraser-Smith, *Love Across Latitudes*, (Gilead Books Publishing, 2015).

person is marrying cross culturally or within their own culture, for either way they still need to learn God's principles for healthy marriage.

Then their family grows even more as they start to have children whom they bring up as believers. That will be a different experience with different sorts of questions relating to identity being asked by the children of BMBs; for example: "Should I be Christian like my parents or Muslim like my cousins?" Or they may decide not to follow any faith as other children do in the West. Therefore it is important to consider the next generation, the BMB's children as well as the BMB themselves. You may play an important role in advising and giving support to the BMB parents, especially if they don't have their extended family around them.

However many believers from Muslim backgrounds find it difficult to find a partner and therefore settling into life may include lots of different types of friendships in and out of church. They may need you to be their family for a long time to come. They may also ask you to help them find a partner, which can be quite a challenge for us in the West.

TIPS TO HELPING BMBS WHO ARE SINGLE:

1 Invite them and involve them in events within the church where they may meet people.

2 Encourage them to build friendships with people around their age group.

3 Encourage and invite them to talk about what they want from a relationship, what their expectations of a relationship would be and how they feel about being single.

4 They may choose to join a Christian online dating agency, support them in this.

5 They may want to go on group holidays where they might make friends with other people their own age.

6 You may be able to help them find conferences and events where they might meet other BMBs.

7 Recognise that people can lead a whole, complete and fulfilled life even outside of marriage.

For everyone life may involve a career or ministry that enables them to be empowered by having their own finances. Many believers of Muslim background have gone on to train as vicars or ministers in the church. Others are involved in serving in the church in pastoral care, support of other BMBs and mission outside the church.

BMBs as gifts to the church

Real belonging for BMBs comes from being invited to be involved in serving in church, being invited to use their gifts and discovering that they are being used by God as part of his body. Believers of Muslim background offer so much to the church!!!

Bruce (Church leader in Oxford)

The British church has learnt a lot and still has a lot to learn from the beautiful commitment that these new Muslim background believers display in their quest for the truth, in their commitment to Christ, and in their devotion to Jesus in their discipleship. We are really amazed and awed at the willing way they say, "If Jesus has done all this for me then I've got to give everything for him".

So here is the challenge for the Western Church now. Frankly, we have become used to being rather comfortable in the West and we are challenged by the depth of commitment and the deep love that these new converts display to us. We don't want to have formal meetings of worship or regular business meetings; we want to know what it is to join a family. That will mean a shared life, deep conversations, planning for the future together and of course food with everything![9]

Long term cultural adjustment

When I first left home and became a believer I rejected everything that was Pakistani as well as rejecting Islam. I had connected the two together, and because of my relationships and feeling trapped within the community, I rejected both.

But then, as I grew in my faith and character, I recognised aspects from Pakistani culture that were still part of me and were good, like respect for and learning from elders, and my sense of humour which is influenced by Pakistani culture. I reclaimed these things and accepted them as part of who I am. Another BMB said that she was a member of white churches for a long time but now has come back to a South Asian church where she feels more at home. Not all BMBs take this route, others may never accept any part of their old culture and that may be fine for them. Acceptance of who they now are is a part of the journey for BMBs and part of the discovery of their new identity in Christ.

The journey with Jesus unfolds through many years. Tim Green calls it the

---

9   *Joining the Family* course.

long journey home. As Hannah found, it's a quest for identity which passes through different phases until the person can finally fit all the pieces together and say, "This is who I am, this is where I belong".

Hannah

Identity shock happens to most of us as teenagers so I guess for me this was compounded by the fact that I lost everything familiar in such a short space of time. But I coped with it initially by rejecting everything that I'd known to be Asian and Muslim and becoming as 'Christian' as I could be, which meant wearing western clothes, cutting my hair, eating pork etc. I was angry with Islam and Muslims. Over time though, I have been able to accept that part of me which is Asian, I still wear western clothes but I love the language and use it often when talking to my husband. Also I enjoy Asian films and humour. I am British Asian and ultimately I am a daughter of God. And belonging to his family, even though it has been at times very hard, is very important to me.[10]

Tim continues:

Psalm 68 says, "God places the lonely in families". What a precious verse that is for those who have lost their birth families as Hannah did. Being part of community helps us find who we are as individuals; it helps us find our home.

We have seen how, on this long journey home, Christ's followers have a vital role to play. Both the wider family of the church and the closer family of a few committed individuals need to walk this journey with their dear brothers and sisters who came from Islam. But we have also stressed how it's not a one-way relationship. Believers of church background have so much to learn from believers of Muslim background, and indeed from believers of Hindu background or atheist background and all backgrounds!

In the end the background melts away because we are one in Christ. It's not that it disappears altogether, how boring that would be! If you mix together all the colours on a palette you just get a muddy brown! No, instead all the colours contribute to a beautiful painting, each with its distinctive contribution. Or it's like threads in a multicoloured tapestry, and praise God that in our generation a sparkling new thread is being woven in for the first time ever. That's the thread of Christ's followers of Muslim heritage in significant numbers. [11]

---

10 Personal conversation.
11 *Joining the Family* course.

Conclusion

We have been on a sort of journey together through this book. We started with thinking about birth community, went from there to thinking about conversion and how it affects the identity of BMBs and their relationship with family. We continued through the difficulties and joys of becoming part of the church community and finding family in the church. We've also talked about mentors joining the BMBs on the path of discipleship and growth and the influence church leaders can have. We've touched upon the gift that BMBs are to the church, and finally we've discussed the long term journey home and the future beyond.

May you know Christ with you as you seek to be part of the journey of believers from Muslim backgrounds. May you know his blessing, wisdom and strength as you walk through the joys and difficulties together. May you know excitement and encouragement as you see Christ's followers of Muslim background grow and go on to live the life that God has for them in all its fullness as members of his family.

Amen

Joining the Family

APPENDICES

APPENDIX 1

Recommended resources

This list of Recommended Resources is arranged according to their topics. We have marked with an asterisk (*) some books and websites we especially recommend. But please bear in mind that any list quickly falls out of date, so you should also search elsewhere including the internet.

This list is not about Islam nor about Christian witness to Muslims. On both these topics there is a vast range of books, audiovisuals, websites and training courses. The *Friendship First* study manual has an Appendix listing some recommended resources, and the *Friendship First leaders guide* has a different, more recent list. The website **answering-islam.org** has much good material with links to more. So too does orientdienst.de (it is in German but right-click for an English translation). But more materials are being created all the time on these topics of Islam and of Christians relating with Muslims.

Instead, the list in this Appendix focusses especially on Muslims who become Christ's followers. Up until now (2016) rather few resources are available specifically on the care, nurture, discipleship and equipping of Christ's followers of Muslim background. Below we list the materials we know about, but please inform us of any gaps, as more resources will be produced in coming years. Please contact us through **joiningthefamily.org** and keep an eye on any further resources listed or uploaded on that site.

Another website **bmbtraining.org** collects in one place various courses designed for discipling and equipping believers of Muslim background. Some courses are uploaded on the site itself and there are links to others. The collection will grow in coming years.

Finally, **mahabbanetwork.com** is an important site for getting and sharing advice, through its secure forum ('The City'). This is a good place to bring your queries and learn from the practical experience of others.

Resources according to topic

1. 'Joining the Family' resources
The following resources were created under the guidance of the Joining the Family core group and are specifically linked with this book.

* Joining the Family Course – six sessions with video and discussion.
* Joining the Family Website - **joiningthefamily.org** – for updated information and responses to queries.
* Joining the Family Seminar materials – to run a seminar in your church – see the website.

2. Muslims finding Jesus
This section is about how and why Muslim people become Christ's followers, and what issues they face afterwards. Some resources describe the overall trends, some tell the story of individuals, and some are based on academic research in a particular context.

2a. Muslims finding Jesus - Trends

* Bradley, Mark. 2014. *Too Many to Jail: the story of Iran's new Christians*. Oxford, UK: Lion Hudson.

* Brother Andrew and Al Janssen. 2007. *Secret Believers*. UK: Hodder and Stoughton.

Council of Ex-Muslims of Britain. See their website ex-muslim.org.uk. There are similar Councils of Ex-Muslims in other countries, with their own websites.

* Garrison, David. 2014. *A Wind in the House of Islam: how God is drawing Muslims around the world to faith in Jesus Christ*. USA: WIGTake Resources.

* Gaudeul, Jean-Marie. 1999. *Called from Islam to Christ: Why Muslims Become Christian*. Crowborough: Monarch Books.

Goode, Reema. 2010. *Which none can shut: remarkable true stories of God's miraculous work in the Muslim world*. Carol Stream, Illinois: Tyndale House Publishers.

Green, Tim. 2011. 'Conversion from Islam to Christianity in Britain', in *Between Naivety and Hostility*, edited by Steve Bell and Colin Chapman. Milton Keynes: Authentic.

Ibn Warraq. 2003. *Leaving Islam: Apostates Speak out*. New York: Prometheus Books.

Miller, Duane and Patrick Johnstone. 2015. 'Believers in Christ from a Muslim Background: A global census', in *Interdisciplinary Journal of Research on Religion*. (www.religjournal.com, Vol 11, Article 10).

* Trousdale, Jerry. 2012. *Miraculous movements: how hundreds of thousands of Muslims are falling in love with Jesus*. Nashville: Thomas Nelson

2b. Muslims finding Jesus – Published research

These publications are based on academic research in particular contexts.

Green, Tim. 2013. 'Beyond the C-Spectrum? A Search for New Models'. *Evangelical Review of Theology* 37 (4): 361–80.

* Greenlee, David, ed. 2006. *From the Straight Path to the Narrow Way*. Milton Keynes, UK: Authentic.

* Greenlee, David, ed. 2013. *Longing for Community: Church, Ummah, or Somewhere in Between?* Pasadena: William Carey Library.

Hefner, Robert. 1993. 'Of Faith and Commitment: Christian Conversion in Muslim Java'. In *Conversion to Christianity: Historical and Anthropological Perspectives on a Great Transformation*, edited by Robert Hefner, 99–125. Berkeley: University of California Press.

Jørgensen, Jonas. 2008. *Jesus Imandars and Christ Bhaktas: Two Case Studies of Interreligious Hermeneutics and Identity in Global Christianity*. New York: Peter Lang.

* Kraft, Kathryn. 2012. *Searching for Heaven in the Real World: A Sociological Discussion of Conversion in the Arab World*. Oxford, England: Regnum.

Larson, Warren. 1998. *Islamic Ideology and Fundamentalism in Pakistan: Climate for Conversion to Christianity?* Lanham, USA: University Press of America.

* Meral, Ziya. 2008. *No Place to Call Home: Experiences of Apostates from Islam, Failures of the International Community*. UK: Christian Solidarity Worldwide.

Syrjänen, Seppo. 1984. *In Search of Meaning and Identity: Conversion to Christianity in Pakistani Muslim Culture*. Finland: Finnish Society for Missiology and Ecumenics.

Willis, Avery. 1977. *Indonesian Revival: Why Two Million Came to Christ*. South Pasadena, CA: William Carey Library.

* Woodberry, Dudley. 2007. 'Why Muslims Follow Jesus'. *Christianity Today* 51: 80–85.

2c. Muslims finding Jesus – Unpublished research

These resources can be hard to access, but are included to indicate the kind of research being carried out. (Here the British system is followed, with 'dissertation' referring to masters level research and 'thesis' for doctorates; in the USA it is the other way around).

Barnett, Jens. 2008. 'Conversion's Consequences: identity, belonging and hybridity amongst Arab Muslim followers of Christ". MA dissertation, Redcliffe College, validated by the University of Gloucestershire.

Cheong, John. 2012. 'The Socio-Religious Identity and Life of the Malay Christians of Malaysia'. PhD thesis, Trinity International University, Deerfield, Illinois.

Green, Tim. 2014. 'Issues of Identity for Christians of a Muslim background in Pakistan'. PhD thesis, SOAS, London University.

Greenham, Anthony. 2004. 'Muslim Conversions to Christ: an investigation of Palestinian converts living in the Holy Land'. PhD thesis, Southeastern Baptist Theological Seminary, USA.

Harper, Des. 2004. 'Why South Asians in Britain come to Christ: factors in the conversion to Christ of people of other faiths'. MA dissertation, All Nations Christian College.

Kronk, Richard. 1993. 'Non-Literary Personal Revelation: the role of dreams and visions in Muslim conversion'. MA dissertation, Dallas Theological Seminary.

Knapstad, Bard. 2005. 'Show Us the Power! A study of the influence of miracles on the conversion process from Islam to Christianity in an Indonesian context'. Masters dissertation, Norwegian Lutheran School of Theology.

Leonard, John. 2006. 'Oasis: an ethnography of a Muslim convert group in France'. PhD thesis, Trinity International University, Deerfield, Illinois.

Maurer, Andreas. 1999. 'In Search of a New Life: conversion motives of Christians and Muslims'. Th. D. dissertation, University of South Africa, Pretoria.

Messenger, Tracey. 1999. 'The Conversion of South Asian Muslims to Christianity in the UK'. MA dissertation, University of Leeds.

Miller, Duane. 2013. 'Living among the Breakage: Contextual Theology-Making and Ex-Muslim Christians'. PhD thesis, University of Edinburgh.

Oksnevad, Roy. 2013. 'An Investigation into the Components of Disharmony in Iranian Muslim Background Churches in the Diaspora'. PhD thesis, Trinity International University, Deerfield, Illinois.

Pope, Valerie. 2013. 'Beyond Welcoming: in search of good practice in welcoming and supporting the growth in faith and discipleship of young Afghan Christians in UK churches'. Masters dissertation, St. John's College, Nottingham. Validated by University of Chester.

Ringler, Lea. 2008. 'Study of the Integration of Muslim Background Believers in France Mission Churches from an Anthropological and Biblical Perspective'. MA dissertation, Fuller Theological Seminary, Pasadena, California.

Schmid, Manfred. 1999. 'Identity Development of Christians from Muslim Backgrounds Living in Germany: a qualitative study'. Unpublished summary of MA dissertation, Columbia International University, Korntal, Germany.

Straehler, Reinhold. 2005. 'Conversion from Islam to Christianity in the Sudan'. M.Th. dissertation, University of South Africa, Pretoria.

Stephenson, John. 2012. 'The Messiah of Honour: the Christology and atonement of followers of *Isa Masih*'. PhD thesis, [University witheld].

Walsh, Thomas. 2005. 'Voices from Christians in Britain with a Muslim Background: stories for the British Church on evangelism, conversion, integration and discipleship". MA dissertation, Birmingham Christian College, validated by University of Wales. (To be uploaded on joiningthefamily.org.)

2d. Muslims finding Jesus - Biographies
Some of these are about finding Christ in Muslim majority countries, some are in Western settings.

Bary, Rifqa. 2015. *Hiding in the light: why I risked everything to leave Islam and follow Jesus*. Colorado Springs: WaterBrook Press.

* Chandler, Paul Gordon. 2007. *Pilgrims of Christ on the Muslim Road: Exploring a New Path between Two Faiths*. Lanham, MD: Cowley Publications.

Habib, Samaa. 2014. *Face to face with Jesus : a former Muslim's extraordinary journey to heaven and encounter with the God of love*. Minneapolis: Chosen.

* Hussain, Khalad. 2012. *Against the Grain*. USA: Xlibris Publishing.

Irwin, Russell. 2010. *The Peanut Butter Man*. Tate Pub and Enterprises Llc.

Masood, Steven. 1986. *Into the Light*. UK: Kingsway.

Naaman, Ghulam and Vita Toon. 1985. *The Unexpected Enemy: A Muslim Freedom Fighter Encounters Christ*. Basingstoke: Marshalls.

* Qureshi, Nabeel. 2014. *Seeking Allah, Finding Jesus*. USA: Zondervan.

* Sangster, Thelma, and Gulshan Esther. 1984. *The Torn Veil: The Story of Sister Gulshan Esther*. UK: Marshalls.

* Shah, Hannah. 2009. *The Imam's Daughter*. London: Rider and Co.

Shah, Ali Husnain. 2016. *The Cost: My Life on a Terrorist Hit List*. Grand Rapids: Zondervan.

* Sheikh, Bilquis. 1978. *I Dared to Call Him Father*. UK: Kingsway.

Wootton, Richard. 1982. *Jesus: More than a Prophet*. Leicester: Inter-Varsity Press.

2e. Muslims finding Jesus - Testimonies in digital media
Many testimonies are available online, see for instance **morethandreams.org** and **answering-islam.org/Testimonies/**. A Google search on 'ex-Muslims for Jesus' and 'Christian ex-Muslims' shows many more.

3. Care and Discipleship
This section keeps 'care' and 'discipleship' together. The section is short for two reasons. Firstly, we have not attempted to explore the huge range of resources on pastoral care and discipleship in general, so the few mentioned here are not carefully selected ones. Secondly, very few materials yet exist on the particular topic of discipleship and care for Christ's followers of Muslim background. If we have missed an important one, please let us know through the website

joiningthefamily.org . We will try to that site information on new resources as they become available.

3a. Care and Discipleship - general

Fraser-Smith, Janet. 1997. *Love Across Latitudes: a workbook on cross-cultural marriage.* (Republished by Gilead Books Publishing, 2015).

Hughes, Selwyn. 2002. *Your Personal Encourager: Biblical help for dealing with difficult times.* UK: Crusade for World Revival.

Whitney, Donald. 1991. *Spiritual Disciplines for the Christian Life.* Colorado Springs: NavPress.

Willard, Dallas. 1988. *The Spirit of the Disciplines*: understanding how God changes lives. San Francisco: Harper and Row.

3b. Care and Discipleship – for believers of Muslim background

Crescent Consultants. 1997. 'Issues of Care and Nurture'. Unpublished report.

Faith in the Fire Associates. 2001. 'Faith in the Fire'. Unpublished consultation report.

Green, Tim. 2014. *Come Follow Me* advisors guide (especially the 'Cultural Clues'). Lulu.com publishers.

Jabbour, Nabil. 2006. *Unshackled and growing: Muslims and Christians on the journey to freedom.* Colorado Springs: Dawson Media.

* Little, Don. 2015. *Effective Discipling in Muslim Communities: Scripture, History and seasoned practices.* USA: Inter Varsity Press.

* Pietzsch, Horst. 2010. *Welcome Home: caring for converts from a Muslim background.* South Africa: SIM.

* Rasiah, C. and Robin Thomson, editors. 2011. *Notes for the Journey: following Jesus, staying South Asian.* UK: South Asian Concern.

3c. Discipleship Courses – for believers of Muslim background
Here we list only some courses specifically for believers of Muslim background, excluding more general resources from which BMBs may of course also benefit. The website **bmbtraining.org** has a growing collection of such courses which are not separately listed below.

* Green, Tim. 2013. *Come Follow Me* course book. Lulu.com publishers.
Hall, Annette. 1999. *Producing Mature Fruit*. Makati City, Philippines: CSM Publishers.

Walsh, Tom and Judi. Discipleship studies for believers of Muslim background. (These are in different stages of readiness; contact them through the joiningthefamily.org website).

4. Muslims in Britain
The following materials give an insight into the different Muslim communities and cultures in Britain, but bear in mind that these continue to evolve all the time. Some of these resources are relevant only in Britain, others more widely.

Ansari, Humayun (2004), *'The Infidel Within': Muslims in Britain since 1800*, London: Hurst and Co.

* Bell, Steve and Colin Chapman, editors. 2011. *Between Naivety and Hostility: uncovering the best Christian responses to Islam in Britain*. Milton Keynes: Authentic.

Contextualising Islam in Britain report. 2009. Cambridge: Centre of Islamic Studies, downloadable from www.cis.cam.ac.uk/CIBPReportWeb.pdf

* Husain, Ed. 2007. *The Islamist: Why I Joined Radical Islam in Britain, What I Saw inside and Why I Left*. London: Penguin.

Hussain, Dilwar. 2004. 'British Muslim Identity'. In *British Muslims between Assimilation and Segregation: Historical, Legal and Social Realities*, edited by Mohammed Sidiq Seddon et al, 83–118. Markfield: Islamic Foundation.

* Lewis, Philip. 1994. *Islamic Britain*, London: I.B.Tauris.

* Lewis, Philip. 2007. *Young, British and Muslim*. London: Continuum.

Mohammed, Shelina Jan. 2014. *Love in a Headscarf*. Aurum Press.
Sardar, Ziauddin. 2004. *Desperately Seeking Paradise*. London: Granta Publications

* Shaw, Alison. 2000. *Kinship and Continuity: Pakistani Families in Britain*. Amsterdam: Harwood Academic.

UK Census data of 2011. Published 2013. www.ons.gov.uk/ons/guide-method/census/2011/census-data/2011-census-data-catalogue/census-data-quick-view/index.html

* Zebiri, Katherine. 2007. *British Muslim Converts: Choosing Alternative Lives*. Oxford: Oneworld.

5. Helping Asylum Seekers

These resources, though mostly originating in Britain, will be of some help in other countries too.

Refugee organisations:

Refugee Council: www.refugeecouncil.org.uk
Refugee Action: www.refugee-action.org.uk
Refugee Support Network: www.refugeesupportnetwork.org
Detention Action: www.detentionaction.org.uk
Boaz Trust: www.boaztrust.org.uk

Christian initiatives and resources in responding to refugees:

For Refugees: www.forrefugees.uk
Capital Mass: www.capitalmass.org.uk/refugee-response
Jesuit Refugee Service (JRS): www.jrsuk.net
Migration and Movement (Lent Study Course): www.weareus.org.uk/resources/migration/
Catholic Church responses to refugees: www.catholicnews.org.uk/Home/Featured/Refugee-Crisis-Open-Your-Hearts

Information and church connections in country of origin:

World Watch Monitor: www.worldwatchmonitor.org
Open Doors: www.opendoorsuk.org
Christian Solidarity Worldwide: www.csw.org.uk/home.htm
Release International: www.releaseinternational.org
Asylum Advocacy Group: britishorthodox.org/tag/aag-asylum-advocacy-group/
Middle East Concern: http://www.globalconnections.org.uk/organisations/middle-east-concern

Housing and campaigns:

Citizens UK: www.citizensuk.org
Positive Action In Housing: www.paih.org/host-a-refugee
The No Accommodation Network: www.naccom.org.uk

City Of Sanctuary: www.cityofsanctuary.org
Places of Welcome: www.placesofwelcome.org

Further Reading:
Council of Ex-Muslims of Britain. 2010. *Apostasy and Asylum in the United Kingdom.*
http://ex-muslim.org.uk/wp-content/uploads/2010/09/
ApostasyandAsylumintheUnitedKingdom.pdf

Houston, Fleur. 2015. *You Shall Love the Stranger as Yourself.* Abingdon: Routledge.

Snyder, Susanna, Joshua Ralston and Agnes Brazal, editors. 2015. *Church in an age of Global Migration: a moving body.* UK: Houndmills and USA: Palgrave Macmillan.

6. Other Resources

6a. Other sources cited in this book
Here we list only sources which were in the book's footnotes but do not already appear in the list above.

Ali, Yusuf. 1938. The Meaning of the Holy Qur'an. A translation into English. The Islamic Foundation.

Berger, Peter and Thomas Luckmann. 1966. *The Social Construction of Reality: a treatise in the sociology of knowledge.* UK: Doubleday.

Heredia, Rudolf. 2007. *Changing Gods: Rethinking Conversion in India.* New York: Penguin.

Kateregga, Badru and David Shenk. 1980. *Islam and Christianity: a Muslim and a Christian in dialogue.* Kenya: Uzima Press.

Lee, Harper. 1960. *To Kill A Mockingbird.* Philadelphia: Lippincott.

Meral, Ziya. 2006. 'Conversion and Apostasy: a sociological perspective'. *Evangelical Missions Quarterly* 42: 508–13.

Ravage, Marcus Eli. 1917. *An American in the Making.* USA: Harper and Brothers. Downloadable from https://archive.org/stream/anamericaninmak00unkngoog#page/n14/mode/2up/

Ten Boom, Corrie. 1982. *Clippings from my notebook*. UK: Thomas Nelson.

The Holy Bible: New International Version. 2011 edition. Grand Rapids: Zondervan.

The Holy Bible: New Living Translation. 1996. Wheaton: Tyndale House.

Wright, N.T. 2011. *Simply Christian*. UK: SPCK Publishing.

6b. Other useful resources

Bell, Steve and Tim Green. 2011. The *Friendship First* DVD course. UK: Interserve.

Christian Muslim Forum. *Guidelines for ethical witness*. www.christianmuslimforum. org/downloads/Ethical_Guidelines_for_Witness.pdf .

honorshame.com – a good website on how the gospel relates to honour and shame.

Muller, Roland. 2006. *The Message, The Messenger and The Community*. Canada: CanBooks.

Rambo, Lewis. 1993. *Understanding Religious Conversion*. New Haven: Yale University Press.

APPENDIX 2

Muslim attitudes to apostasy in Britain

The following extract is from Tim Green's chapter with this title, in the book edited by Steve Bell and Colin Chapman, *Between Naivety and Hostility: Uncovering the best Christian responses to Islam in Britain* (Authentic, 2011). It is reproduced with permission.

Although the traditional attitudes to apostasy still influence grassroots Muslim opinion, yet Islamic scholars have increasingly called for their review, suspension or even abolition in Britain today. The chapter cites some examples of this up until 2010. Further work is needed to bring the picture up to date.

Apostasy in Islamic tradition

Islamic attitudes to apostasy developed early and hardened quickly, not to be challenged in any significant way until modern times. The consensus of the centuries was almost unanimous: apostates are traitors and deserve execution.

Islam's formative period

This stern attitude derives only in part from the Quran, which in fact is quite ambiguous on whether apostates should be punished in this life or only by God in the afterlife. More clear-cut were Muhammad's words, as reported in several Hadith including the well-known saying 'he who changes his religion, kill him'.[1] Attitudes to apostasy continued to harden immediately after Muhammad's lifetime, as the nascent Muslim state fought to re-assert its authority over dissident Arab tribes. Whether their rebellion was religious or political, the net result was the same: to weld together firmly the concepts of political and religious allegiance. Loyalty to Allah meant loyalty to His ruler on earth. Rejection of one necessarily implied rejection of the other, so apostasy spelt treason.

And so down through history, Muslim societies have tended to view religious apostates as social renegades and political traitors. Far from being unique to Islam, such a stance is typical of collectivist cultures including pre-modern Christendom. Religion is not a private choice, but rather a tribal or ethnic identity label. A person switching over to the religion of a different ethnic group, especially an enemy group, is perceived as rejecting their heritage and bringing shame upon their whole community. It upsets the social order. It needs to be crushed.

Thus in all schools of Islamic law, Sunni and Shia, the unambiguous penalty for sane male apostates is death. The jurists differed over who is qualified to pronounce the sentence, and on what to do with female apostates or the insane, and on how much time to allow an apostate to change their mind, and on what constitutes apostasy anyway. But the principle of capital punishment was clear-cut and almost unopposed. Not content merely with capital punishment, the jurists also applied civil penalties, such as the automatic dissolution of an apostate's marriage and the confiscation of his or her property.[2]

In practice the penalty was rarely applied down the centuries, simply because so few Muslims ever converted to Christianity.

The colonial era

From the early nineteenth century onwards, European colonial rule allowed missionaries and Christian literature to have some influence in Muslim lands. Although the numbers converting to Christianity remained small, attitudes began to change among some Muslim scholars exposed to western education, such as Muhammad Abduh. They began to argue that rejection of Islam need not automatically imply rebellion against the government.

Others, even in the modern era, continued to argue that all apostasy is treason. Abu Ala Maududi (probably Islamism's most influential ideologue in the twentieth century), argued that freedom of religion in Islam means freedom to enter, not to leave. For him, the interests of the Islamic state take precedence over those of the individual, so 'a state has the right to use force to... crush those segments which insist on breaking away'.[3] Such extreme statements were perhaps an embarrassment to even Maududi's own followers, who declined to translate them into English, but he was not alone in making them.

Twentieth century human rights discourse

Pressure for change increased with the human rights provisions enshrined in the 1948 United Nations Declaration of Human Rights. Most Muslim governments assented to the U.N. Declaration, while harbouring doubts over article 18 which, by asserting a person's 'freedom to change his religion or belief', directly challenged the Islamic law of apostasy.

Islamic versions of human rights declarations later modified this freedom significantly.[4] For instance, the Universal Islamic Declaration of Human Rights (1981), while maintaining a studied ambiguity in its English version, is clear enough in the original Arabic that 'forsaking the Islamic community' is forbidden. However, it should be borne in mind that this and other 'Islamic Declarations' have not carried great influence in practice.

Further change in the twenty-first century

Within the last few years, internationally recognised Muslim leaders have increasingly started to state publicly and boldly that apostates should not be punished by death. In 2002 the world's foremost Islamic university Al Azhar, under its late imam Sheikh Tantawi, declared the death penalty for apostasy to be 'null and void'. Other leaders followed suit, prompted especially by the widely-publicised news in 2006 that a convert in Afghanistan had been initially sentenced to death. In response the views of more than one hundred notable Muslim scholars who oppose this penalty for apostasy were published on the 'Apostasy and Islam' website. Their worldwide list of names is quite impressive and includes several who are prominent in Britain.[5]

In addressing international audiences, these scholars spoke in a clear-cut way. But those of them based in Muslim-majority countries needed to perform a balancing act, as Egypt's grand mufti Ali Gomaa found in 2007 when he first informed an international forum that apostasy should only be punished if combined with treason, and then later assured irate Muslims at home that apostasy and treason are linked anyway! In Qatar in 2006, the influential Yusuf al-Qaradawi supported the death sentence for apostasy, albeit hedged around with caveats. A 2009 conference of Islamic jurists meeting in the Middle East was unable to take an agreed position on punishment for apostasy.

So, at an international level the doors of *ijtihad* (creative interpretation) are starting to creak open, though slowly and fitfully. What about Britain in particular?

Contemporary debate in Britain

In 2007, Channel 4 screened a 'Dispatches' documentary on Muslims converting to Christianity in Britain. On the programme senior clerics Suhaib Hasan of the Shariah Council of Great Britain, and Ibrahim Mogra of the Muslim Council of Britain, were confronted with evidence that some converts face violent intimidation from Muslims. Both were adamant that there should be no punishment for apostates. Afterwards Mogra reiterated to a Muslim audience that an apostate 'should be left alone without being intimidated at all', for 'he has chosen Hell-fire by his own choice'.[6]

In 2008 an insightful Radio 4 programme 'Could I stop being a Muslim?' asked a range of Muslim leaders in Britain whether they think the death penalty still applies for apostates. Usama Hassan, an imam with a Cambridge PhD, argued that

'the classical law of apostasy in Islam is wrong and based on a misunderstanding of the original sources, because the Quran and the teaching of the Prophet don't actually talk about a death penalty for apostasy.'

Haras Rafiq, leader of the Sufi Muslim Council, agreed.

However, other interviewees were equally adamant that the death penalty still applies in principle. 'There are legislations and rulings which remain eternally and they will remain up until we perish and the world itself perishes', asserted Abu Khadijah, a Wahabi running an Islamic bookstore in Birmingham. A Deobandi lecturer, teaching jurisprudence at an imam's training college in Britain, similarly stated that the 'unanimous consensus among the jurists' is for the death penalty.[7]

Between these two extremes, most interviewees sought space in the middle ground. They agreed that apostates in Britain today should certainly not be punished, but were unwilling to sweep aside altogether the consensus of the centuries. For, as Dr. Hisham Hellyer (now a fellow at Warwick University) explained,

'When you have an agreement in Islamic law, it's something that cannot just be taken off the books.. The classic punishments can be suspended under certain circumstances, commuted under certain circumstances, even theoretically inapplicable... but it can't simply be taken off the books, because that this tantamount to your saying that all the authorities that came before you, that agreed in such massive terms, were wrong and misguided'.

Scholars taking this middle ground seek ways to explain why the penalty for apostasy could still be valid in theory but would not apply in Britain today: either because it is not an Islamic state, or because there is no perfect Islamic ruler to pronounce sentence (a Shia view), or because apostasy should only by punished when combined with treason.

In 2008-09, a widely-acclaimed project under Cambridge University brought together twenty six Muslim scholars, activists, community leaders and academics to discuss what Islam means in Britain today. Their report makes the breathtakingly bold assertion that Islam:

'prohibits discrimination against apostates... It is important to say quite simply that people have the freedom to enter the Islamic faith and the freedom to leave it.'[8]

In 2009, the Muslim Christian Forum drew up a set of 'ethical guidelines for Christian and Muslim witness in Britain'. This is a landmark document, for it was agreed by recognised leaders from both faith communities, and it tackles head on the question of conversion. The guidelines state that 'we should recognise that people's choice of faith is primarily a matter between themselves and God', and that

'whilst we may feel hurt when someone we know and love chooses to leave our faith, we will respect their decision and will not force them to stay or harass them afterwards'.[9]

In 2010 a Christian convert challenged a gathering of imams and clergy to recognise that some in Britain who convert from Islam are treated very badly by the Muslim community. Afterwards some of the Muslim leaders told her privately that they were deeply upset and shocked by what she said, and that they would go back to their communities to challenge this attitude to converts.

Thus, change is in the air. A growing number of mainline Muslim leaders in Britain are now affirming - clearly, corporately and unambiguously - the right of individuals to leave Islam without being punished or harassed.

But has this new lenient approach by Islamic scholars yet made any difference to Muslim attitudes on the street? To this we now turn.

How do British Muslims treat apostates in practice?

A startling poll result

In 2007 in a Policy Exchange poll, no less than 36% of British Muslims aged 16 to 24 believed that apostates should be killed. Considering that most of these young people had been brought up and educated in a liberal society, this response was surprising indeed. It may reflect more what they feel *should* be said to an interviewer, in terms of giving the correct Islamic answer, than what they have carefully considered for themselves. Still less does it indicate any action they would actually carry out. But it seems clear that scholars' more liberal attitudes have not yet 'trickled down' to street level, at least among certain sectors of Muslim society. Significantly, this age group of British Muslims gave more radical answers than their elders across a whole range of questions in the poll, and this probably reflects their more self-consciously 'chosen Islam' in contrast to the 'cultural Islam' of the previous generation.[10]

Do some converts face physical danger?

I know of no cases of converts in Britain being murdered for their Christian faith. However, there have certainly been recent attempts at murder. In July 2009 two Afghan converts in Heathrow's main detention centre were told by other inmates 'if we are sent back to Afghanistan on the same flight, we will kill you before we land there'. Indeed, one of them reports that during a riot in their wing, thirty angry Afghans tried to break into his room and kill him.[11]

Another 2009 incident took place in the Bradford area, when a Pakistani convert to Christianity was very badly beaten with baseball bats by five young men, including his brother and nephews. Bricks had previously been thrown through his windows and his family threatened. Surprisingly the assailants were let off with a suspended sentence, and were later to be seen boasting of their impunity. Another Pakistani convert in Bradford, Nissar Hussein, similarly believes that the authorities made a complacent response to the death threats and property damage which he and his family endured over several years until he was eventually forced to move house.[12]

So, severe persecution can take place in Britain today. At risk are converts who live in solidly Muslim urban enclaves, where disaffected second generation Muslim youth adopt an aggressively Islamic identity and claim the local turf. Where Islam's 'territory' is staked out within prisons or detention centres, violent intimidation may be impossible to escape.[13] South Asian females can be another high-risk category, because of cultural codes of honour which punish them more harshly than males for bringing shame on families.[14]

Is this typical for converts in Britain?

It is important to stress that cases of violent persecution are not typical in Britain. They represent just one extreme from a whole spectrum of Muslim responses. Most converts are 'merely' (though this is still devastating) verbally abused by their Muslim families, perhaps ejected from their homes, and disowned by the community. Rather typical would be the experience of a British Pakistani friend of mine, who was scornfully told by her relative "Don't you realise, that by becoming a Christian you have abandoned your roots, your heritage and your family name?"

At the other extreme are those cases where the Muslim family is neutral or even positive towards the convert. Another British-born Pakistani lady was, by her mid-twenties, in a fearful state. Divorced and back in her family home, she was so plagued by depression and demonic oppression that she was on the verge of suicide. But after she found Christ, the changes in her life were so positive and dramatic that her Muslim family members did not object to her new faith. She continues in good relationship with them.

In between these two extremes come the more typical family reactions: almost always negative, almost always hurtful, but rarely life-threatening.

This is confirmed by two field studies. Tom Walsh interviewed sixteen former Muslims, mostly of South Asian ethnicity and all living in Britain. Their relatives expressed extreme disappointment ('in their grief they didn't eat'), anguish ('my mum cried buckets and buckets') and concern for their honour in the community (to the extent of jeopardising siblings' marriage prospects). They reacted by condemning or isolating or ignoring or expelling their errant family member who had brought such shame upon them.[15]

Des Harper interviewed twenty three converts from Islam in Britain. He found that family reactions, while negative, were overall less severe than in the published conversion accounts arising from Muslim majority countries. Moreover, despite the initial rupture or strain, relationships tend to improve over time. Almost half of Harper's sample reported that their Muslim community came eventually to accept or even respect them; of the others, most continued to be viewed with suspicion, some were ignored or ostracized, and only a few underwent ongoing hostility. Generally his Iranian interviewees faced less difficulty than those from the Indian subcontinent.[16]

These findings fit with my own experience, that even when initial family response is hostile, some degree of reconciliation is likely after several years.

1   This hadith is in Sahih Bukhari, volume 4, book 52, number 260, found in http://www.usc.edu/schools/ college/crcc/engagement/resources/texts/muslim/hadith/bukhari/052.sbt.html
2   I have only given a brief summary. For more detail, see The Maranatha Community, *Apostasy: An Overview* (2006); Ziya Meral, *No Place to Call Home: Experiences of Apostates from Islam, Failures of the International Community* (UK: Christian Solidarity Worldwide, 2008); Patrick Sookhdeo, *Freedom to Believe: Challenging Islam's Apostasy Law* (USA: Isaac Publishing, 2009).
3   Abul 'Ala Mawdudi *The Punishment of the Apostate According to Islamic Law* (Urdu *Murtadd ki Saza Islami Qanun men* (1942), translated into English by Syed Silas Husain, publisher not given, c.1995))
4   Further helpful detail is found in Colin Chapman *Islam and the West: Conflict, Coexistence of Conversion?* (UK: Paternoster, 1998) chapter 5, and Ziya Meral, No Place to Call Home, chapter 3.
5   These names include Zaki Badawi, Ziauddin Sardar, Abdul Hakim Winter, Ruqaiyyah Waris Maqsood and Tariq Ramadan, all of whom have spoken clearly against the punishment of apostates. See http:// apostasyandislam.blogspot.com for the full list and for their respective opinions.
6   reported in *The Muslim Weekly*, 21 September 2007, p. 2

7   The radio programme obtained this quote from the website www.muftisays.com but the particular individual is not named.
8   *Contextualising Islam in Britain*, Cambridge: Centre of Islamic Studies, 2009, p.75, downloadable from www.cis.cam.ac.uk/CIBPReportWeb.pdf .
9   The ten guidelines are downloadable from www.christianmuslimforum.org/downloads/Ethical_Guidelines_for_Witness.pdf .
10 For more on attitudes and trends among British born Muslims, see Philip Lewis, *Young, British and Muslim*, (London: Continuum, 2007).
11 The account is given in Interserve's *Go* magazine, 2010/1, pg.5.
12 His account appears in newspapers and in Sookhdeo, *Freedom to Believe*.
13 For a March 2010 report on alleged intimidation by Muslim gangs in British prisons, see http://news.bbc.co.uk/1/hi/uk/8558590.stm .
14 'South Asian' refers to those whose ethnic origins are from Pakistan, India or Bangladesh. 6The 2006 Maranatha report, p.30, lists several cases of attempted murder of Pakistani females, and one actual case where the girl was sent back to Pakistan and shortly afterwards died in an improbable 'accident'.
15 Thomas Walsh, 'Voices from Christians in Britain with a Muslim Background: Stories for the British church on evangelism, conversion, integration and discipleship'. (MA dissertation, University of Birmingham, 2005).
16 Harper, Des (2004). 'Why South Asians in Britain come to Christ: Factors in the conversion to Christ of People of other Faiths'. (MA dissertation, All Nations Christian College, 2004).

APPENDIX 3

Underlying issues in lifestyle change

Tom and Judi Walsh have contributed the following material. It builds on what they wrote in Chapter 8 of this book, on Life Structure, recognising that what lies 'above the surface' in our lives can only really be changed when what lies 'beneath the surface' is properly addressed.

Above and below the surface

Often changing our behaviour is far more than superficial. Our lives are like an iceberg. We only show ourselves or see in others the ten percent above the waterline. The other ninety percent is below the surface and is unseen. What we observe is the behavior; what is hidden is the reason for this behaviour, the emotions and feelings, the thoughts, and deep down at the bottom the driving force, the story we tell ourselves, the 'life commandment' at the bottom of it all.

Life commandments are the things we tell ourselves which we learned at such a young age we don't even remember. Typical life commandments would be things like:

"I am worthless."
"I am not clever."
"My sister should do what I want."
"Everyone should be punctual."
"I am hopeless at Maths."
"Feelings are not important."
"Be a good boy"

We have found the 'Iceberg Model' helpful in identifying and addressing life commandments.

The iceberg: Identifying life commandments

The model begins by asking "What is the situation you want to change?" Responses should be specific and may be written in the chart on the next page.

OLD BEHAVIOUR   NEW BEHAVIOUR

OLD BEHAVIOUR	NEW BEHAVIOUR
1. Actions or behaviour	8. New plan of action and behaviour
2. Feelings & emotions	7. Feelings & emotions
3. Thoughts	6. Thoughts
4. My life commandment	5. God's truth

Starting with the specific situation you want to change:

Step 1 identifies the behaviour you show at present that needs to change. This is the tip of the iceberg you and everyone else sees.

Step 2 you go below the water and think about the feelings and emotions that fuel that behaviour, the hidden part.

Step 3 going deeper still, you try to identify the thoughts that feed the emotions.

Step 4 takes you to the bottom of the iceberg where you try to see what the life commandment is that has been driving you.

Step 5 moves you across to ask what is God's truth about this situation? For example if your life commandment is something like "I am worthless," God's truth will be "You are my creation, chosen and precious. You are a child of God and of immense value." It could be a specific verse of Scripture.

Step 6 you are beginning to move upwards again as you think about what God says about you and what does that mean for your life. What thoughts does God's perspective bring to you?

Step 7 asks you to consider how you feel about these amazing truths, the emotions they now raise, and finally back up above the waterline

Step 8 enables you to be clear about the new behaviour and plan of action to move forward.